THE RISE OF THE ARISTOLOGIST

Arehitecting Power That Outlives You

— By Roger Gore —

First published 2026

Table of Contents

INTRODUCTION

The Day a New Doctrine Was Born

There comes a moment in the life of every builder when success is no longer enough. Income is no longer enough. Recognition is no longer enough. The applause fades quickly and the trophies gather dust, but the question that lingers is whether what has been built will remain. I reached that moment after years of studying ownership, distribution, authority, and structure. I had taught that control begins with access. I had shown that hustle must mature into architecture. Yet I could not ignore what I was witnessing in business, in families, and in communities. Power was being used, but it was not being designed to last.

I began to observe a pattern. Talented entrepreneurs built impressive brands that struggled to survive a leadership transition. Families accumulated wealth but lacked governance, education, and succession planning, resulting in conflict or decline. Communities rallied around charismatic figures but failed to institutionalize progress in a way that would sustain momentum. The pattern was clear. We had learned how to rise. We had not learned how to remain.

The word Aristocrat existed long before this book. Historically it described those who held power or status. In modern language it often evokes privilege or rank. Yet as I examined the concept, I recognized a limitation. An Aristocrat uses power. An Aristocrat commands influence. An Aristocrat benefits from position. But that word did not capture the responsibility of designing systems that outlive the individual. It described position but not permanence.

Language shapes thought. Thought shapes behavior. If we lack a word for responsibility, we often fail to embrace it fully. That realization compelled me to create a new word. Aristologist. I did not create it casually. I created it because the moment required it. Aristologist names the individual who architects generational power. Aristologist identifies the leader who studies structure, succession, governance, and institutional design. Aristology names the doctrine behind that discipline. It is philosophy that teaches how to transform personal success into permanent infrastructure.

This is not branding. This is my responsibility. This is not a motivational phrase. This is a structural framework. Deeply that the most dangerous form of power is power that dies with its owner. Wealth without education for heirs becomes confusing. Influence without governance becomes conflict. Ownership without succession becomes fragmented. If we do not design what we build to survive us, then we have built monuments to ourselves instead of foundations for those who follow.

The first book in this journey taught that you must control the channel. If you do not control distribution, you are dependent on those who do. The second book taught that you must move from hustling within systems to architecting them. But this book completes the cycle. It asks you to think beyond your lifetime. It demands that you consider not only how high you can rise, but how long your impact can endure. Channel control gives leverage. Architecture gives stability. Aristology gives permanence.

As I reflected on my own journey, I understood that creating a new doctrine is not about ego. It is about clarity. Every generation faces a decision. Will we consume what was handed to us, or will we construct something stronger for those who come after us? I do not believe generational strength happens by accident. It happens by design. It requires teaching. It requires documentation. It requires governance. It requires intention. That belief became the heartbeat of Aristology.

I often say at speaking engagements that success is impressive, but permanence is powerful. I say that income feeds a year, but structure feeds a century. I say that building a business is ambition, but building an institution is responsibility. These lines are not clever slogans. They are reminders. They are anchors to a way of thinking that prioritizes continuity over charisma.

The Rise of the Aristologist is not about creating an elite class. It is about creating disciplined architects of power who understand their obligation to family, community, and future generations. It is about transforming temporary achievement into transferable systems. It is about ensuring that the sacrifices of one generation do not have to be repeated by the next because the blueprint was never written.

True revolution is not loud. It is structured. True power is not flashy. It is durable. True leadership does not end with personal success. It extends into generational stewardship. I created the words Aristologist and Aristology because our era demands a new category of leaders. Leaders who think beyond quarterly earnings and immediate applause. Leaders who understand governance, succession, and institutional continuity. Leaders who accept what they build must survive them.

If you embrace this doctrine, you are not simply pursuing

wealth. You are pursuing permanence. You are not simply seeking authority. You are constructing infrastructure. You are not simply rising. You are ensuring that others will not have to start from the ground you once stood upon. That is the difference between an Aristocrat and an Aristologist. One uses power. The other architects do it.

This book is an invitation to step into that higher responsibility. It is an invitation to move from success to stewardship. It is an invitation to participate in a revolution that will not be televised because it is happening in boardrooms, in family councils, in community institutions, and in disciplined minds. If we accept this call, the promise will be fulfilled not in a single lifetime but across many. That is the rise. That is the doctrine. That is Aristology.

master the use of power, yet if that power remains dependent on his presence alone, its lifespan is limited.

Across industries and across generations, the same pattern appears. Founders build through sacrifice and clarity. Successors inherit without comprehensive preparation. Conflicts emerge where governance is undefined. Decisions become reactive rather than strategic. What once stood firm begins to fracture. Outside observers often attribute decline to personality or circumstance, but the root cause is structural. Power that dies was never designed to live.

The Pattern of Generational Erosion

Research on wealth preservation reveals a consistent pattern of decline across generations. The first generation builds. The second maintenance is. The third struggles. This is not destiny, but it is frequent. It occurs when acquisition is prioritized over institutionalization. It occurs when values are assumed rather than documented. It occurs when succession is treated as an uncomfortable conversation rather than a strategic priority.

Wealth without education becomes consumption. Influence without governance becomes tension. Ownership without transfer planning becomes fragmentation. None of these outcomes are mysterious. They are predictable when structure is neglected. The Aristologist studies these patterns not to criticize success, but to fortify it. He understands that permanence must be intentional. He does not rely on hope or assumption. He relies on architecture.

Success that depends on one personality is temporary. Success embedded in structure becomes permanent. That principle must be embraced fully before the doctrine of Aristology can be applied effectively.

The Responsibility of Stewardship

Achievement brings visibility, but stewardship brings responsibility. When growth stabilizes and authority is established, a deeper obligation emerges. The leader must begin to think beyond immediate expansion and consider continuity. Stewardship requires humility because it demands acknowledgment that no individual remains forever. It requires foresight because it stretches vision beyond a single lifetime. It requires discipline because it involves documentation, governance, and education that may not provide immediate reward.

Governance delayed weakens continuity. Succession postponed increases risk. Documentation neglected invites confusion. The Aristologist understands that permanence must be woven into the fabric of growth. It cannot be postponed until later seasons. It must be constructed alongside expansion.

Control builds position. Architecture builds stability. Continuity builds legacy. This progression represents maturity in leadership. It moves from immediate success to generational strength. It transforms ambition into infrastructure.

Designing for Absence

One of the most powerful exercises a leader can undertake is to design for the day he is not present. This is not pessimism. It is prudence. In that future moment, will decisions align with documented values. Will disputes be resolved through established processes? Will successors understand not only the mechanics of leadership but the philosophy behind it? Will assets remain protected within structures designed to withstand transition.

The Aristologist writes constitutions. He establishes councils. He clarifies governance roles. He educates heirs early. He creates systems that reduce ambiguity. He understands that leadership without structure creates dependency, while leadership embedded in structure creates resilience.

Design for the day you are not there, and your presence will echo through the systems you created. That echo is legacy.

The Birth of a Doctrine

The creation of the word Aristologist was not casual. It emerged from recognition that the existing language lacked precision. Aristocrat described one who uses power. It did not describe one who architects its survival. Aristology names the study and discipline of designing generational authority. It elevates responsibility from performance to permanence.

This is a quiet revolution. It does not seek attention. It seeks durability. It does not promise instant transformation. It demands intentional construction. It invites leaders to move beyond applause into architecture. It challenges them to think in decades rather than quarters, in generations rather than cycles.

True revolution redesigns assumptions. Aristology redesigns how power is understood, protected, and transferred.

Closing Reflection and Charge

Examine what you have built. Look beyond revenue and recognition. Evaluate governance, succession, documentation, and education. Ask whether your leadership has been institutionalized or merely demonstrated. Ask whether your family understands the structure behind the wealth. Ask whether your organization can function with clarity in your absence.

Do not leave this chapter inspired but unchanged. Inspiration without structure is another form of temporary power. Begin documenting principles. Begin formalizing governance. Begin preparing successors intentionally. Begin thinking in decades rather than seasons.

If it is worth building, it is worth protecting across generations. Power that dies was never designed. Design it so it lives.

And remember this as you move forward.

Build beyond yourself.

Design beyond your lifetime.

Let your power move like poetry in motion and stand like stone in time.

Arise. Architect. Endure.

Personal power, no matter how disciplined, is limited by human capacity. There are only so many hours in a day, only so much attention one person can distribute, only so much emotional bandwidth available for decision making. When growth continues but structure does not evolve, the leader becomes the bottleneck of progress. This is not immediately obvious. It appears first in small delays, unresolved tensions, repetitive decision cycles, and increasing dependency on one voice. Over time, these patterns accumulate and reveal a ceiling that was always present but rarely acknowledged.

The ceiling does not accuse the leader of incompetence. It reveals the absence of architecture.

The Weight of Centralization

Centralization is often necessary in early stages. When a business is young or a family enterprise is forming, strong centralized decision making can provide clarity and direction. However, what serves early growth can restrict long term expansion if not adjusted intentionally. When all significant authority rests with one individual, the system becomes vulnerable to fatigue, bias, and eventual transition shock.

Centralized power may appear efficient, yet it carries hidden risk. When others are not trained to think strategically, when processes are not documented, and when governance is not formalized, knowledge remains concentrated rather than distributed. Concentrated knowledge is powerful while active but fragile when disrupted. Distributed knowledge supported by structure creates resilience.

The Aristologist recognizes that leadership is not weakened by structure but strengthened by it. Establishing advisory boards, councils, documented procedures, and defined succession pathways does not remove authority. It multiplies it. It allows decisions to be guided by principles rather than by impulse. It ensures continuity of direction even when personalities change.

The serious reader must understand this clearly. If leadership cannot function without constant intervention from one person, it is not institutional. It is personal.

The Psychological Barrier to Evolution

One of the most significant barriers to breaking through the Aristocrat's ceiling is psychological attachment to indispensability. Many leaders derive identity from being the central figure. Being needed reinforces purpose. Being the final authority confirms status. The thought of distributing power may want to surrender significance.

Yet true significance is not measured by how indispensable you are in the present. It is measured by how stable the system remains in your absence. Indispensability without structure produces fragility. Replaceable leadership within strong architecture produces endurance.

This transition requires emotional maturity. The leader must shift from seeking validation through direct control to seeking legacy through systemic strength. It requires confidence to empower others without fear of diminishing one's own authority. It requires humility to document processes that others will one day use independently.

Leadership that cannot be shared cannot survive.

When Growth Outpaces Governance

Rapid expansion can disguise structural weakness. As revenue increases and influence broadens, energy focuses on opportunity rather than organization. Teams grow quickly, yet governance may lag. Assets multiply, yet protection mechanisms remain informal. The outward image of success expands, yet inwardly, clarity may erode.

When growth outpaces governance, tension eventually surfaces. Decision conflicts become more frequent. Roles blur. Accountability weakens. Strategic direction becomes reactive rather than deliberate. These symptoms often appear subtle at first, but they signal that structure has not evolved alongside scale.

The Aristologist studies growth patterns with discipline. He understands that each new level of expansion requires corresponding refinement in governance. Increased revenue demands stronger financial oversight. Expanded leadership teams require clearer role definitions. Multi-generational wealth requires documented stewardship education. Growth without governance eventually reaches instability.

There is a principal worth engraving in the mind. Scale without structure collapses under its own weight.

The Illusion of Stability

Success can create the illusion that stability is permanent. When systems function smoothly under current leadership, it may appear that no additional architecture is necessary. However, stability that relies heavily on one personality is not stability. It is alignment around presence.

Consider what happens when that presence is removed suddenly or gradually. If there is no documented transition plan, if successors are uncertain about authority boundaries, if governance guidelines are incomplete, instability quickly replaces alignment. Stability must be designed to withstand absence, not merely presence.

The Aristologist anticipates disruption before it occurs. He builds contingency plans. He establishes leadership pipelines. He creates clear documentation of mission, values, and operational frameworks. He trains successors intentionally rather than assuming readiness will develop naturally.

Stability that survives transition is true stability.

From Command to Continuity

The Aristocrat commands. The Aristologist continues. This distinction represents evolution rather than opposition. Command is necessary. It initiates momentum. Continuity sustains it. Command establishes authority. Continuity protects it across time.

Continuity requires intentional systems. It requires governmental structures that define decision rights and responsibilities. It requires formal education for those who will inherit leadership roles. It requires financial frameworks that protect assets from mismanagement or internal conflict. It requires communication channels that preserve unity during transition.

The Aristologist does not abandon ambition. He elevates it. He refuses to accept that decline across generations is inevitable. He studies examples of families and institutions that have endured for centuries and extracts principles from their design. He understands that longevity is rarely accidental. It is structured.

Chapter Reflection & Strategic Notes

The Rise of the Aristologist

CHAPTER THREE

THE THREE GENERATION COLLAPSE

There is a pattern so consistent across cultures, industries, families, and institutions that it can no longer be dismissed as coincidence or misfortune. It is the pattern of the three-generation collapse. The first generation builds. The second generation maintains. The third generation struggles. Wealth fades. Influence fractures. Institutions are weakening. What once appeared permanent becomes a memory. The tragedy is not that this happens. The tragedy is that it continues to happen despite being predictable.

The first-generation builder is always forged in adversity. Scarcity shapes discipline. Uncertainty sharpens focus. Risk strengthens resolve. The builder understands cost because he has paid it personally. He knows what it means to operate without safety nets. Every dollar earned carries weight. Every opportunity seized carries consequence. This generation builds with urgency because failure is not theoretical. It is immediately. In this environment structure is often secondary to survival. Expansion matters more than documentation. Growth matters more than governance. The builder is consumed with proving that stability is possible.

Yet within this intensity lies a blind spot. The builder assumes that the next generation will understand what he understands simply because they inherit what he built. He assumes that proximity will transfer perspective. He assumes that wealth will carry wisdom. But perspective does not transfer biologically. Discipline does not transfer automatically. Responsibility does not transfer passively. If the architecture of governance is not written, taught, and reinforced, the next generation receives assets without understanding structure.

The second generation inherits a different reality. It grows closer to stability than to scarcity. It may respect the sacrifices of the first generation, but it did not experience them in the same way. It operates from a foundation that feels more secure. If governance has been formalized and doctrine has been documented, this generation can strengthen and expand what was built. But if structure remains informal and authority remains centralized, the second generation often operates in ambiguity. It may protect what exists but struggle to scale it responsibly. Without clear decision-making frameworks, disagreements become personal. Without documented mission and values, direction becomes subjective. The burden shifts from expansion to interpretation.

By the third generation the distance from original sacrifice widens further. If intentional education has not been embedded into family or institutional culture, wealth may be perceived as normal rather than earned. Influence may be treated as entitlement rather than stewardship. Leadership may feel like inheritance rather than responsibility. This is not a moral indictment of the third generation. It is a structural observation. Without deliberate preparation, exposure to abundance without exposure to architecture creates vulnerability.

The three-generation collapse is not caused by laziness alone. It is caused by absence of design.

Wealth without governance becomes unstable. Ownership without defined structure becomes fragmented. Influence without succession planning becomes contested. Assets without education become liabilities. The pattern repeats not because families lack intelligence but because they lack infrastructure. The builder focused on creating opportunities. The maintenance generation focused on preserving comfort. No generation focused intentionally enough on institutionalizing doctrines.

Aristology emerges at this precise failure point.

The doctrine of Aristology was born from the recognition that generational decline is preventable but not accidental. It requires intentional design. It requires leaders who think beyond their lifetime. It requires architecture that separates ownership from daily management when necessary. It requires governance charters that clarify voting authority and dispute resolution. It requires financial literacy programs embedded into family culture. It requires councils, boards, and documented mission statements. It requires humility to imagine absence and discipline to prepare for it.

The Aristocrat uses power effectively. The Aristologist architects it so that it survives.

This distinction is not cosmetic. It is foundational. The Aristocrat excels in execution. He negotiates skillfully. He commands rooms. He builds enterprises. But if his authority

responsible.

Generations do not fall by accident. They fall by absence of design.

Chapter Reflection & Strategic Notes
The Rise of the Aristologist

CHAPTER FOUR

THE MOMENT OF A NEW WORD BECAME NECESSARY

There are moments in intellectual history when existing language becomes insufficient for emerging responsibility. The evolution of ideas has always required the evolution of vocabulary. Political revolutions gave birth to new words that described new systems of governance. Economic shifts introduced terminology that captured new models of exchange and value. Scientific breakthroughs demanded language that could articulate discoveries that had never before been understood. In each of these cases, the creation of a new word did not represent vanity. It represented necessity. It represented the recognition that old categories could no longer contain new understanding.

The same phenomenon occurs in leadership and generational design. For centuries, the word aristocrat described a person who occupied a position of elevated authority. Historically it was associated with inherited rank, with lineage, with power concentrated in specific bloodlines. Over time the word evolved and began to describe individuals who operated at a high standard or exercised refined authority within their environment. Yet even in its modern use, the word carried limitations. It described one who possessed power or used power effectively. It did not describe one who engineered power for permanence. It did not describe the discipline required to protect authority across generations. It did not describe the science of designing continuity.

The inadequacy of language becomes clear only when a leader confronts repeated structural failure. When observing families whose wealth dissolved despite extraordinary beginnings, when examining companies that dominated markets but collapsed within decades of leadership transition, when studying institutions that were celebrated in one era and forgotten in the next, a pattern emerges that cannot be ignored. The problem is not ambition. The problem is not intelligence. The problem is not even moral in many cases. The problem is structural absence.

In ancient Rome, political power often centered around powerful individuals whose authority seemed unshakable during their lifetime. Yet without institutional reforms strong enough to survive the ambitions of successors, the Republic gave way to instability and eventual transformation. In more modern contexts, industrial magnates built vast empires in steel, oil, and finance. Some families preserved wealth across centuries by establishing trusts, boards, and governance councils. Others fractured because ownership fragmented without coordination and succession planning remained informal. History provides both warning and blueprint. It shows that power exercised without design evaporates. It also shows that power embedded within structured systems can endure.

The recognition that something deeper was missing began not as a branding exercise but as a structural reckoning. It became clear that describing a leader as an aristocrat was incomplete. The Aristocrat commands authority. The

measure it effectively.

The necessity of Aristologist emerged because the world has enough performers and not enough architects of permanence. It emerged because generational collapse is too common to ignore. It emerged because success without structure is temporary power disguised as achievement.

The word was not created for novelty. It was created because history demanded it.

As this chapter closes, understand this clearly. Language shapes leadership. Name the responsibility and you begin to live it. Refuse to name it and you risk repeating the patterns of the past.

Power that is not engineered will eventually erode. Permanence begins the moment you decide to design it.

Chapter Reflection & Strategic Notes
The Rise of the Aristologist

CHAPTER FIVE

USING POWER VERSUS ENGINEERING IT

Throughout history there have always been individuals who knew how to use power effectively. They mastered negotiation. They understood leverage. They commanded loyalty. They influenced markets and shaped institutions. Their names often dominate headlines and textbooks. Yet for every figure who wielded power skillfully, there are far fewer who ensured that the structures supporting that power endured beyond their lifetime.

Using power is visible. Engineering power is often invisible. Using power produces immediate results. Engineering power produces sustained stability. Using power depends on strength and timing. Engineering power depends on foresight and systemization.

The distinction between the two disciplines is foundational to Aristology. A leader may use power to acquire assets, expand influence, and dominate competitors. However, if the mechanisms that protect those assets are weak, if succession remains informal, if governance is undefined, then the power used today becomes vulnerable tomorrow.

Consider the example of corporations that grew rapidly

Chapter Reflection & Strategic Notes
The Rise of the Aristologist

CHAPTER SIX

WHY INCOME IS NOT INFRASTRUCTURE

There is a dangerous illusion that often accompanies financial success. It is the belief that income alone represents stability. When revenue increases, when assets accumulate, when lifestyle improves, it feels as though permanence has been secured. Yet history repeatedly demonstrates that income is not infrastructure. Income is flow. Infrastructure is foundation. Income can fluctuate with markets, leadership changes, economic downturns, or internal conflict. Infrastructure, when properly designed, absorbs fluctuation and preserves continuity.

The distinction between income and infrastructure is one of the most critical concepts within Aristology. Income is the result of activity. Infrastructure is the result of design. Income reflects present performance. Infrastructure protects future permanence. When leaders confuse income with stability, they build wealth without reinforcing the systems necessary to preserve it.

Consider the difference between a profitable company and a durable institution. A profitable company may generate significant revenue under strong leadership. It may dominate its market for a season. Yet if that profitability depends entirely on one decision maker, if governance is informal, if succession planning is absent, and if ownership structures are fragmented, the company remains vulnerable. Profitability does not equal permanence. Revenue does not equal resilience.

Infrastructure begins when income ends. Infrastructure includes governance structures that define authority and accountability. It includes legal entities that protect assets from fragmentation or liability. It includes succession frameworks that clarify leadership transition. It includes education systems that prepare future stewards. It includes financial discipline that balances expansion with preservation.

Throughout history, many individuals accumulated extraordinary income yet left little lasting institutional impact because infrastructure was neglected. Conversely, some leaders built moderate income streams but established robust institutions that endured across centuries. The difference was not talent. It was structured.

Income is temporary by nature. Markets change. Consumer behavior shifts. Technology evolves. Economic cycles rise and fall. Infrastructure anticipates these realities and builds flexibility into governance and ownership. Without infrastructure, income must constantly be rebuilt from scratch with each new disruption. With infrastructure, income may fluctuate, but the system remains intact.

Another misconception is that infrastructure can be postponed until income reaches a certain threshold. Leaders often say they will formalize governance once revenue stabilizes or once expansion slows. This delay creates vulnerability. Infrastructure should develop alongside income, not after it. Waiting until complexity increases makes retrofitting structure more difficult and more disruptive.

The Aristologist treats infrastructure as primary rather than secondary. He understands that wealth without structure invites erosion. He ensures that legal frameworks are clear. He defines roles within organizations and families explicitly. He establishes councils or boards that review decisions independently. He creates documentation that guides behavior even when he is not present.

Infrastructure also extends to culture. Cultural infrastructure includes documented values, mission statements, and expectations that shape behavior across generations. Without cultural infrastructure, identity weakens. Without identity, decision making becomes inconsistent. Infrastructure preserves coherence.

The difference between income and infrastructure can be illustrated through physical analogy. Income is like rainfall. It can nourish growth temporarily. Infrastructure is like irrigation systems and reservoirs. It ensures that nourishment continues even when rainfall is inconsistent. Without irrigation, growth depends entirely on weather conditions. Without infrastructure, wealth depends entirely on favorable circumstances.

Financial literacy is another element of infrastructure. When heirs inherit income without understanding financial principles, preservation weakens. Infrastructure requires education programs that ensure comprehension of budgeting, investment strategy, risk management, and long horizon planning. Wealth transferred without understanding becomes fragile.

The Aristologist also distinguishes between visible wealth and protected wealth. Visible wealth includes properties, businesses, and lifestyle. Protected wealth includes trust, holding structures, diversified assets, and legal safeguards.

Visible wealth can be admired. Protected wealth can endure.

Infrastructure is not glamorous. It does not generate applause. It requires paperwork, meetings, documentation, and discipline. It demands patience. Yet it is infrastructure that separates temporary prosperity from generational strength.

Examine whether your current income streams are supported by structural protection. Are ownership shares consolidated strategically? Are leadership roles defined clearly? Is succession formalized? Are financial strategies diversified and documented? Are governance meetings held consistently with recorded minutes? These questions determine whether income stands on solid ground or shifting sand.

Income is the product of effort. Infrastructure is the product of foresight.

Leaders who fail to understand this distinction often find themselves rebuilding repeatedly after disruption. Leaders who prioritize infrastructure find that even when income fluctuates, their foundation remains stable. Stability allows recovery. Stability allows continuity. Stability allows growth across generations.

The Aristologist does not despise income. He respects it enough to protect it. He recognizes that accumulation without architecture is incomplete. He designs structures that transform revenue into resilience.

As you reflect, ask whether your financial success has been matched by structural development. Consider whether your systems can withstand transition, market shifts, or internal disagreement. If the answer is uncertain, infrastructure requires immediate attention.

Let this principle guide you forward. Revenue creates

opportunity. Infrastructure preserves it.

And remember this clearly.

Income is what you earn. Infrastructure is what remains.

Chapter Reflection & Strategic Notes
The Rise of the Aristologist

CHAPTER SEVEN

OWNERSHIP IS THE BEGINNING, NOT THE END

For many leaders, ownership represents the pinnacle of achievement. The moment an individual moves from employee to owner, from participant to principal, from contributor to controller, a psychological shift occurs. Ownership feels like arrival. It signals autonomy, authority, and control. It represents liberation from dependence. In the context of the earlier doctrine, building the channel and becoming the authority centers around this concept of ownership. Yet Aristology demands a deeper understanding. Ownership is not the end of the journey. It is the beginning of responsibility.

Ownership without structure is power without protection. It grants access but does not guarantee endurance. It creates opportunity but does not automatically create permanence. Many individuals have achieved ownership only to discover that without governance, succession planning, and structural clarity, what they own remains vulnerable.

The assumption that ownership equals security is one of the most persistent illusions in economic life. A business owner may believe that holding majority shares ensures stability. A property owner may assume that title guarantees continuity. A founder may believe that control of equity secures legacy. Yet ownership that is not embedded within durable frameworks can be diluted, contested, mismanaged, or fragmented.

Throughout history, entire enterprises have collapsed not because ownership was absent but because ownership was unmanaged. When shares were divided among heirs without voting agreements, decision paralysis followed. When control was concentrated without succession planning, instability emerged at transition. When legal protections were informal or incomplete, external forces disrupted continuity.

Ownership is power, but it is raw power. Infrastructure refines it.

The Aristocrat celebrates ownership because it provides authority in the present. The Aristologist studies ownership because he understands its fragility without design. He asks not only who owns but how ownership is structured, how it is transferred, how it is protected, and how it is governed.

Consider the difference between individual ownership and institutional ownership. An individual may own assets outright, but if those assets are not placed within structured entities such as holding organizations or trusts with defined governance, they remain exposed to fragmentation or dispute. Institutional ownership provides continuity beyond the individual lifespan. It consolidates assets under defined rules. It prevents impulsive division. It preserves strategic direction.

Ownership must also be aligned with purpose. Without documented mission and defined values, ownership can drift into opportunism. When heirs inherit shares without understanding vision, they may prioritize short term liquidity over long term stability. The Aristologist embeds ownership within doctrine. He ensures that those who hold equity understand the philosophy that governs it.

Another dimension of ownership responsibility involves education. Ownership is not merely possession. It is stewardship. Stewardship requires competence. Financial literacy, governance understanding, and strategic awareness must accompany equity. Without education, ownership becomes a burden rather than a privilege.

Ownership also introduces ethical responsibility. When leaders own enterprises that employ communities, their decisions impact livelihoods beyond their immediate circle. Ownership therefore carries public consequences. The Aristologist acknowledges this and structures governance to balance profit with stability and social responsibility.

There is also the matter of emotional attachment. Owners often equate identity with possession. Letting go of direct control can feel like loss. Yet Aristology reframes ownership as layered rather than centralized. Direct operational control may transition while ownership remains structured within defined parameters. This allows continuity without stagnation.

Ownership is the first step toward authority, but without architecture, it is incomplete. It is the foundation upon which governance, succession, and institutionalization must be built.

Reflect on your current ownership structures. Are they consolidated strategically? Are voting rights defined clearly? Is succession of equity formalized? Are dispute resolution mechanisms documented? Are ownership roles accompanied by education requirements? These questions determine whether ownership will endure or erode.

The most significant transition in this chapter is

psychological. Ownership must be viewed not as entitlement but as obligation. It is not merely the right to benefit. It is my duty to preserve and multiply responsibly.

When ownership is structured properly, it becomes a stabilizing force across generations. When it is unmanaged, it becomes the seed of fragmentation.

The Aristologist understands that ownership is the beginning of the journey into permanence. It marks the moment when authority shifts from opportunity to responsibility.

As this chapter closes, let this truth settle deeply.

Owning something gives you control today. Structuring ownership gives it life tomorrow.

Ownership opens the door. Architecture keeps it open.

Chapter Reflection & Strategic Notes
The Rise of the Aristologist

CHAPTER EIGHT

DESIGN BEFORE DOMINANCE

There is a pattern that has repeated itself across centuries of leadership, conquest, commerce, and influence. Those who pursue dominance before design often rise quickly and fall just as swiftly. Those who commit to design before dominance may rise more deliberately, but they endure with far greater stability. The difference between the two approaches is not ambition. It is architecture.

Dominance is visible. It commands attention. It produces headlines. It signals power. It is measured in market share, territory, influence, valuation, and applause. Design, however, is quieter. It is measured in governance frameworks, succession documents, ownership structures, institutional clarity, and documented values. Dominance attracts followers. Design sustains institutions.

History offers countless illustrations of this principle. Military leaders who conquered vast territories without building administrative systems capable of maintaining them saw their empires fracture upon their death. Political figures who seized control without institutional reform left unstable regimes behind. Entrepreneurs who expanded aggressively without internal governance structures often faced collapse when complexity exceeded personal capacity. In each case, dominance preceded design. Momentum replaced structure. The result was temporary glory followed by structural erosion.

The Aristocrat often pursues dominance instinctively. Excellence drives him to win, to scale, to capture market advantage, to expand influence. There is strength in this instinct. Without driving, nothing is built. Without ambition, no authority is gained. Yet Aristology introduces necessary discipline. Design must precede dominance. Architecture must undergo expansion. Infrastructure must support influence before it multiplies.

Design begins with clarity. It demands a written mission that transcends personality. It requires documented governance structures that define authority and accountability. It insists upon ownership frameworks that protect assets from fragmentation. It includes succession planning that anticipates transition long before it becomes urgent. It embeds education systems that prepare future leaders while current leaders remain active.

When dominance comes without these elements, fragility hides beneath strength. Complexity grows faster than coordination. Influence expands faster than oversight. Revenue increases faster than financial discipline. Under such conditions, growth becomes vulnerable.

Consider the example of institutions that have endured for centuries. Universities, long standing family enterprises, financial institutions with multigenerational governance, and cultural foundations often share one trait. They were designed intentionally before or during expansion. Their founders established charters. They defined decision making bodies. They clarified roles. They embedded culture in writing. They anticipated succession. Because of this design, leadership could change without dissolving the mission.

Contrast this with enterprises built around a single charismatic leader who delayed governance because growth felt urgent. As the organization scaled, informal processes became strained. Decision making bottlenecks emerged. Conflict increased because expectations were undefined. When transition occurred, the absence of design became undeniable. What seemed powerful was exposed as centralized rather than institutional.

Design before dominance requires humility. It requires leaders to slow down when acceleration feels exciting. It requires acknowledging that growth without guardrails can be destructive. It requires asking difficult questions before expansion, such as whether governance systems can support additional complexity, whether succession is documented clearly, and whether ownership structures prevent dilution.

The Aristologist recognizes that unstructured dominance creates risk. He does not suppress ambition. He channels it through architecture. He asks how expansion will be governed, how new leaders will be integrated, how culture will be preserved, and how accountability will be maintained. He ensures that success is scalable because it is structured.

Design also includes cultural design. As organizations grow, culture can drift if not documented. Early values rooted in sacrifice and discipline may fade as comfort increases. The Aristologist writes culture into constitutions, codes of conduct, and mission statements. He reinforces it through leadership training and governance review. He ensures that growth does not dilute identity.

Financial design is equally critical. Before dominance through expansion, financial frameworks must be defined. Clear capital allocation policies, reinvestment strategies, diversification plans, and risk management protocols prevent overextension. Many leaders chase scale without evaluating sustainability. Design prevents ambition from becoming instability.

There is also psychological design. The Aristologist prepares successors mentally for leadership long before authority transfers. He allows them to observe governance meetings. He teaches decision making philosophy. He clarifies expectations. Dominance that transitions without psychological preparation creates insecurity and conflict.

The discipline of design before dominance separates momentary power from enduring influence. It shifts the question from how fast we can grow to how strong our foundation is. It moves attention from visibility to viability. It prioritizes resilience over rapid applause.

Examine your current trajectory. Are you expanding faster than you are structuring? Are new initiatives launched without governance review? Is succession discussed informally rather than documented formally. Are ownership stakes protected or vulnerable? Is culture preserved intentionally or assumed to persist automatically? These questions reveal whether dominance is supported by design.

The Aristologist refuses to allow excitement to outrun architecture. He commits to building the foundation before adding additional floors. He understands that structural weakness is not obvious during growth but devastating during stress.

Design is not delayed. It is preparation. It is not caution born of fear. It is foresight born of responsibility. It does not prevent dominance. It strengthens it.

When dominance follows design, growth becomes

sustainable. When design follows dominance, repair becomes necessary. The order determines the outcome.

As this chapter closes, remember this clearly.

Design what you build before you expand what you build.

Architecture first. Authority second.

Dominance that is not designed will decline. Dominance that is engineered will endure.

Chapter Reflection & Strategic Notes
The Rise of the Aristologist

CHAPTER NINE

SUCCESSION IS STRATEGY, NOT SENTIMENT

There is no more revealing in the life of a leader than the moment he must confront his own replacement. Expansion feels powerful. Growth feels validating. Authority feels stabilizing. Succession feels unsettling. It forces a confrontation with mortality, relevance, control, and ego. It shows whether leadership was institutional or personal. It reveals whether design preceded dominance or whether dominance relied entirely on presence.

Across generations and industries, institutions rarely collapse at the height of performance. They collapse at transition. They fracture when authority shifts without clarity. They weaken when ownership transfers without governance. They divide when emotion replaces structure. Succession is not the ceremonial passing of a title. It is the most strategic decision in the lifespan of any institution.

The greatest mistake leaders make is confusing succession with inheritance. Inheritance is distribution. Succession is transfer of responsibility within structure. Inheritance can occur automatically. Succession must be engineered. Inheritance is a legal event. Succession is a strategic process.

When leaders treat succession as a sentimental gesture rather than a structural strategy, instability follows.

History offers sobering lessons. Monarchies that failed to define succession rules experienced civil wars. Corporations that lacked documented leadership criteria faced boardroom conflict and shareholder uncertainty. Family businesses that relied on assumed understanding saw sibling rivalry dissolve decades of accumulated strength. In each case, the absence of strategic succession planning created vulnerability at the precise moment stability was needed most.

Sentiment is powerful. It influences decision making quietly. Leaders may choose successors based on emotional closeness rather than competence. They may avoid difficult conversations to preserve temporary harmony. They may delay planning because discussing succession wants to admit decline. These emotional impulses are human, but unstructured emotion at transition is dangerous.

The Aristologist confronts this reality early. He recognizes that succession must be defined while strength is stable, not when crisis forces urgency. He documents criteria for leadership roles clearly. He separates ownership from operational authority when necessary. He ensures that competence is evaluated objectively. He integrates governance bodies into the decision-making process to reduce bias.

Succession must begin long before transfer occurs. It begins with mentorship. It continues with structured exposure to decision making. It requires evaluation based on performance rather than assumption. It demands that successors understand not only operational mechanics but philosophical doctrine. Without doctrinal alignment, authority may be exercised without continuity.

One of the most destabilizing forces in succession is ambiguity. When roles are not clearly defined, competing interpretations emerge. When voting rights are unclear, conflict intensifies. When expectations are not documented, resentment grows. Ambiguity creates emotional friction because individuals fill informational gaps with personal assumptions.

Strategic succession eliminates ambiguity. It clarifies timelines. It defines qualifications. It establishes review processes. It documents authority boundaries. It communicates transition plans to stakeholders transparently. Clarity reduces fear. Structure reduces rivalry.

Another critical distinction must be made between preparation and designation. Many leaders designate successors without adequately preparing them. Title without training creates insecurity. Authority without mentorship invites error. Preparation requires deliberate investment of time and responsibility. It includes exposure to governance meetings, financial review sessions, conflict resolution processes, and strategic planning discussions.

Succession also demands humility from the current leader. Letting go of centralized control challenge's identity. Leaders accustomed to being the final authority must learn to trust structure over instinct. They must allow successors to make decisions and experience consequences within defined frameworks. Without this gradual transfer of responsibility, sudden transition becomes destabilizing.

The Aristologist understands that succession is not a single event but a phased progression. Observation leads to participation. Participation leads to partial authority. Partial authority leads to full leadership within governance. Each stage is documented and evaluated. This progression reduces shock and strengthens confidence.

Financial succession must also be addressed with discipline. Ownership structures should be consolidated within entities that prevent fragmentation. Voting agreements should be formalized. Trust structures may be utilized to align long term vision with asset distribution. Without financial structure, succession becomes liquidation rather than continuation.

The psychological dimension of succession cannot be ignored. Heirs must be prepared emotionally for leadership. They must understand the weight of responsibility. They must recognize that authority is not privilege but obligation. They must internalize that stewardship extends beyond personal benefit to institutional stability.

Leaders must also confront favoritism. Emotional preference cannot replace competence evaluation. Succession is based solely on bloodline without regard for capability undermines continuity. The Aristologist establishes objective criteria that apply consistently. This protects both the successor and the institution.

Silence is often the enemy of successful succession. Difficult conversations are postponed because they feel uncomfortable. Yet delay amplifies risk. Unexpected events expose unprepared systems. The Aristologist refuses to postpone clarity. He initiates dialogue early. He invites questions. He documents decisions.

Consider the cost of unplanned succession. Market confidence declines. Employees question directions. Family members dispute authority. Legal battles emerge. Wealth diminishes through conflict rather than market loss. Reputation suffers. All because strategy was replaced with sentiment.

Now consider the alternative. Succession documents are

written and reviewed regularly. Successors are trained deliberately. Governance councils participate in evaluation. Ownership structures prevent dilution. Transition is announced clearly. Stakeholders understand the process. Confidence remains intact.

The difference is not luck. It is architecture.

Examine your current approach honestly. Have you defined leadership criteria clearly? Have you formalized succession timelines? Are successors being mentored intentionally? Are governance bodies integrated into the process? Are financial structures prepared for transfer? If not, sentiment may be governing where strategy should lead.

Succession is not about stepping aside. It is about ensuring what you built stands stronger when you do.

The Aristologist does not wait for crisis to expose weakness. He anticipates transition and designs stability. He treats succession as a strategic discipline equal in importance to growth, acquisition, or innovation.

As this chapter closes, let this truth settle firmly.

Love your family enough to structure their future.

Affection without architecture fractures.

Succession is not emotional generosity. It is a strategic responsibility.

Design the transfer before time demands it.

Chapter Reflection & Strategic Notes

The Rise of the Aristologist

CHAPTER TEN

THE MIND OF THE ARISTOLOGIST

Before institutions are built, before governance is documented, before succession is structured, there is a mindset that must be formed. Structures are external reflections of internal discipline. Systems are manifestations of thinking. Permanence begins in the mind long before it appears on paper. The Aristologist is not defined first by what he builds but by how he thinks.

The mind of the Aristologist operates on a different time horizon than the average leader. While many think in quarters, product cycles, or election terms, the Aristologist thinks in decades and generations. He evaluates decisions by asking not only whether they create immediate advantage but whether they strengthen continuity. He refuses to separate ambition from responsibility. He measures success not solely by growth but by durability.

This mental discipline requires patience in a culture obsessed with speed. Modern environments reward rapid expansion and immediate visibility. Social proof, valuation spikes, and public recognition create pressure to accelerate. The Aristologist resists acceleration when it outpaces architecture. He understands that speed without structure amplifies risk. He is willing to move deliberately when others rush because he prioritizes permanence over applause.

Another defining characteristic of this mindset is emotional restraint. The Aristologist does not allow ego to dictate structure. He does not build systems that revolve exclusively around his personality. He recognizes that charisma is powerful but temporary. He intentionally reduces dependency on his presence by codifying processes and distributing authority within governance frameworks. This requires humility because it acknowledges that no individual, regardless of strength, is permanent.

The Aristologist also practices intellectual honesty. He studies patterns of collapse without denial. He examines failed enterprises and fractured families not with judgment but with curiosity. He asks what structural weaknesses were ignored. He identifies where sentiment replaced strategy. He extracts lessons before repeating mistakes. This capacity to confront uncomfortable truths separates emotional leadership from architectural leadership.

Long horizon thinking also reshapes financial behavior. The Aristologist resists excessive consumption that undermines capital stability. He prioritizes reinvestment, diversification, and asset protection. He understands that visible wealth is less important than protected wealth. He designs capital structures that can withstand economic cycles rather than relying on favorable conditions.

There is also a relational dimension to this mindset. The Aristologist views family not merely as a private bond but as an institution that requires governance. He recognizes that affection does not eliminate complexity. As families grow, perspectives multiply. Without structure, differences escalate. The Aristologist introduces councils, documented values, and decision frameworks to protect relationships from unmanaged conflict. He understands that love without structure can unintentionally create instability.

Discipline defines his daily behavior. He documents decisions. He schedules governance reviews. He mentors successors intentionally. He studies financial statements with seriousness. He communicates expectations clearly. These habits may appear administrative to observers, but they are foundational. Permanence is rarely dramatic. It is constructed through consistent disciplined action.

The Aristologist also embraces responsibility beyond personal wealth. He recognizes that institutions influence communities. Employment, philanthropy, cultural leadership, and economic stability ripple outward. When institutions collapse, communities suffer. Therefore, his design extends beyond private interest. He structures organizations to serve sustainably. He embeds accountability mechanisms that protect stakeholders beyond immediate family.

A critical element of this mindset is resistance to entitlement. The Aristologist does not assume that prior success guarantees future relevance. He remains vigilant. He updates governance structures as complexity increases. He educates successors continuously. He reviews strategy regularly. Complacency is treated as vulnerability. Stability is maintained through attention.

Fear of irrelevance often drives leaders to cling to control. The Aristologist reframes relevance. He understands that true relevance is measured by what functions without him. When systems operate effectively in his absence, his leadership has succeeded at the highest level. He derives satisfaction not from being indispensable but from being foundational.

The mind of the Aristologist also values documentation as

protection. Memory is unreliable and interpretation varies over time. Written doctrine creates clarity that survives emotion. Governance charters reduce conflict. Succession plans reduce speculation. Ownership agreements reduce fragmentation. Documentation transforms vision into enforceable structure.

There is courage in this mindset. It takes courage to confront mortality without denial. It takes courage to initiate succession conversations early. It takes courage to evaluate theirs objectively. It takes courage to prioritize infrastructure over immediate gratification. The Aristologist embodies this courage quietly but consistently.

He also understands compounding influence. Decisions made today shape opportunities for grandchildren not yet born. He recognizes that generational wealth is not measured solely in currency but in access, education, and stability. His thinking therefore extends beyond himself. He sees himself as a steward within a longer continuum rather than the center of it.

The Aristologist rejects the illusion that dominance guarantees endurance. He knows that empires have collapsed under leaders who believed their strength was permanent. He studies history not to admire conquest but to understand continuity. He extracts lessons from institutions that endured centuries and applied those principles intentionally.

This mindset reshapes identity. The Aristocrat is proud of victory. The Aristologist is proud of design. The Aristocrat commands rooms. The Aristologist builds rooms that command respect long after he is gone. The Aristocrat celebrates acquisition. The Aristologist celebrates consolidation and protection.

Examine your own thinking honestly. Do you measure success by visibility or by viability? Do you delay governance because growth feels urgent. Do you assume heirs will understand responsibility without formal education? Do you avoid succession discussions because they feel uncomfortable. These patterns reveal whether mindset aligns with permanence.

The transformation from Aristocrat to Aristologist begins internally. It begins when ambition is disciplined by foresight. It matures when ego is subordinated to architecture. It solidifies when permanence becomes the primary metric of achievement.

The mind of the Aristologist is not reactive. It is anticipatory. It does not chase opportunity without evaluating structure. It does not celebrate growth without reinforcing governance. It does not transfer wealth without transferring wisdom.

As this section closes, understand this clearly. Structures reflect thought. If the mind is short term, institutions will be fragile. If the mind is generational, institutions will endure.

Permanence is first a decision of perspective before it becomes a document of governance.

Think beyond yourself and you will build beyond yourself.

Chapter Reflection & Strategic Notes
The Rise of the Aristologist

CHAPTER ELEVEN

ARISTOLOGY DEFINED

Every enduring discipline in history began as an observation before it became a doctrine. Political theory began when leaders recognized patterns of governance and failure. Economic theory began when thinkers studied exchange, scarcity, and value across time. Military strategy was formalized only after repeated victories and defeats revealed predictable structures beneath chaos. In the same way, Aristology did not emerge from imagination alone. It emerged from studying generational rise and generational collapse. It emerged from recognizing that power without structure evaporates, that wealth without governance fragments, and that ownership without education erodes across time.

Aristology is the doctrine of permanent power. It is the disciplined study and architectural design of authority that outlives the individual who creates it. It is not concerned merely with acquisition. It is concerned with continuity. It does not focus only on influence. It focuses on institutionalization. It does not celebrate momentary dominance. It engineers generational endurance.

To define Aristology properly, one must first understand what it is not. It is not elitism. It is not inherited entitlement. It is not social hierarchy based on exclusion. It does not depend on birthright. Aristology is accessible to any leader who accepts responsibility for permanence. It is a discipline of design, not a privilege of lineage. It requires thoughtfulness, humility, foresight, and structure.

At its core, Aristology rests on a fundamental premise. Power that is not engineered will decline. This premise is supported by centuries of evidence. Families that accumulated vast fortunes without consolidating ownership structures often watched wealth divided into inefficiency. Enterprises that scaled rapidly without formal governance frequently collapsed when complexity exceeded personal capacity. Political regimes built around personalities rather than institutions fractured upon transition. The pattern is consistent across geography and industry.

Aristology therefore defines power differently. Power is not simply the ability to command resources or influence outcomes. Power is the ability to preserve authority across transitions. It is the capacity to maintain direction when leadership changes. It is the stability of mission when personalities evolve. It is the resilience of assets when markets fluctuate. Under Aristology, power is measured by durability rather than dominance.

This doctrine introduces several structural commitments. The first is documented governance. Governance transforms informal authority into defined systems. It clarifies roles, voting thresholds, succession criteria, and conflict resolution procedures. It reduces ambiguity and prevents emotional interpretation from replacing documented process. Without governance, authority is vulnerable to dispute. With governance, authority is institutional.

The second commitment is structured ownership. Ownership must be consolidated strategically to prevent fragmentation. Holding structures, trusts, defined equity agreements, and voting protocols protect unity of direction. Aristology recognizes that multiplication of heirs without consolidation multiplies instability. Ownership must therefore be engineered intentionally.

The third commitment is education as infrastructure. Heirs and successors must understand financial literacy, governance philosophy, and institutional history. Wealth transferred without wisdom becomes unstable. Authority granted without training becomes fragile. Education ensures that stewardship replaces entitlement.

The fourth commitment is cultural continuity. Values, mission, and identity must be documented and reinforced. Culture shapes decision making across generations. Without written doctrine, culture drifts. With doctrine, culture anchors continuity.

Aristology is not static. It requires periodic review. Governance documents must evolve as complexity increases. Ownership structures must be evaluated as families expand. Leadership pipelines must be strengthened continuously. The doctrine demands vigilance rather than complacency.

Historically, institutions that endured centuries often embraced these principles implicitly, even if they did not name them. Family banking dynasties established councils and trusts. Universities codified charters and boards. Religious institutions preserved doctrine through written canon and structured leadership succession. Each example reflects Aristological thinking before the term existed. The difference now is that the doctrine is named, formalized, and made intentionally.

Aristology also reframes legacy. Legacy is not measured by monuments or recognition. It is measured by stability. It is not measured by wealth at the time of death. It is measured by wealth that continues responsibly after death. It is not measured by influence for one generation. It is measured by institutional coherence across multiple generations.

Doctrine demands emotional discipline. Leaders must confront mortality without denial. They must initiate succession planning while strong. They must allow government bodies to participate in oversight. They must mentor successors deliberately. Ego must yield to architecture. This psychological transformation is as important as legal structure.

Aristology also emphasizes community responsibility. Institutions influence broader economic ecosystems. When generational stability exists, communities benefit from sustained employment, philanthropy, and leadership continuity. When collapse occurs, communities absorb the shock. Therefore, the doctrine carries social weight beyond private benefit.

There is also an economic dimension to Aristology that must be understood clearly. Capital compounds when protected within structure. Fragmented capital weakens compounding power. Institutionalized capital can invest strategically across decades. Short-term consumption undermines long-term stability. Aristology aligns financial behavior with generational thinking.

To define Aristology succinctly yet completely, it can be described as the disciplined architecture of generational authority, combining governance, ownership consolidation, succession strategy, education, and cultural continuity to transform temporary power into permanent institutions.

This definition is not theoretical. It is operational. It demands documentation, planning, review, and humility. It requires leaders to think beyond their own timeline. It insists that success is incomplete unless it is preserved.

Examine your current structure honestly. Is governance documented formally? Are ownership shares consolidated intentionally? Are successors trained systematically? Is culture written and reinforced? Are transition plans explicit rather than implied. These questions determine whether Aristology is philosophy or practice in your life.

The significance of defining Aristology formally is this. What is named can be pursued deliberately. What is undefined remains accidental. By defining this doctrine, leaders gain a framework for evaluating decisions and building institutions intentionally.

The world does not lack ambitious leaders. It lacks architectural leaders. Aristology answers that deficiency.

As this chapter closes, understand that doctrine is not mere language. Doctrine shapes behavior. Once permanence becomes the metric, every decision changes.

Power exercise is impressive. Power engineering is enduring.

The doctrine of permanent power begins the moment you decide to design what will outlive you.

Chapter Reflection & Strategic Notes
The Rise of the Aristologist

CHAPTER TWELVE

THE ARCHITECTURE OF PERMANENCE

Every structure that endures is built upon principles that were invisible long before the structure was visible. Skyscrapers rely on foundations buried beneath the ground. Cathedrals that stand for centuries rest on calculations made by architects who understood weight, pressure, and stress long before the first stone was placed. Institutions are no different. The permanence of power depends on architecture that is often unseen by the public but decisive in moments of transition. Aristology is not satisfied with defining permanence. It demands its construction.

The architecture of permanence begins with foundation. Foundation in institutional terms refers to governance. Governance establishes the rules by which authority operates. It defines how decisions are made, who has the right to vote, how conflicts are resolved, and how leadership transitions occur. Without governance, power rests in personality. With governance, power rests in principle. This distinction is fundamental. Personality fades. Principle can be codified.

Governance must be written. Informal understanding cannot withstand generational complexity. Families expand. Businesses grow. Stakeholders multiply. Memory becomes unreliable. Interpretation varies. Written governance documents, charters, constitutions, bylaws, and agreements transform assumption into clarity. They remove ambiguity before ambiguity becomes dispute.

Yet governance alone is insufficient if ownership remains fragmented. The second pillar of architectural permanence is structured ownership. Ownership defines who holds equity, but architecture defines how that equity functions. Without consolidation mechanisms, generational expansion dilutes influence and complicates decision making. Holding companies, trusts, and defined equity classes are not instruments of control for their own sake. They are stabilizers that protect direction across time.

Structured ownership prevents liquidation through internal disagreement. It ensures that long term strategy cannot be overturned impulsively by temporary sentiment. It protects the mission from being compromised by fragmentation. The Aristologist studies ownership structures as carefully as financial statements because he understands that unstructured equity is silent instability.

The third structural layer is succession planning integrated within governance. Succession cannot be a ceremonial announcement. It must be embedded within architecture. Clear criteria for leadership roles, documented evaluation processes, mentorship systems, and phased authority transfer ensure that transition strengthens rather than weakens institutions. Succession planning is not about replacing one individual with another. It is about transferring responsibility within an intact system.

Architecture also requires financial durability. Institutions that endure manage capital strategically. They diversify assets, establish reserve funds, and implement disciplined reinvestment policies. They avoid excessive leverage that exposes the entire structure to single points of failure. Financial architecture acknowledges economic cycles and prepares for volatility rather than assuming perpetual growth.

Cultural architecture is equally vital. Institutions collapse not only because of financial mismanagement but because of cultural erosion. When shared values are not documented and reinforced, identity weakens. The Aristologist codifies mission and values clearly. He ensures that culture is taught deliberately to emerging leaders. Culture becomes an anchor during transition, preventing drift.

Another essential component of permanence is layered oversight. Oversight bodies such as advisory boards, independent directors, or councils introduce accountability that transcends individual preference. These bodies provide perspective, challenge assumptions, and protect missions. Oversight does not undermine authority. It strengthens it by distributing wisdom.

Architecture must also anticipate stress. Just as engineers calculate how structures respond to earthquakes or storms, institutional architects must anticipate economic downturns, leadership disputes, market disruption, and generational conflict. Contingency planning becomes part of design. Emergency succession protocols, dispute resolution mechanisms, and crisis governance procedures prevent panic during pressure.

The Aristologist recognizes that architecture is not static. It evolves as complexity increases. Early-stage governance may be simple. As scale expands, structures must mature. What protected ten employees may not protect one thousand. What governed a small family may not govern an extended network across continents. Permanence requires adaptation without abandoning core principles.

One of the most overlooked aspects of architectural permanence is documentation discipline. Minutes from governance meetings, formal resolutions, strategic plans, and financial reports create institutional memory. Memory allows continuity even when individuals change. Without documentation, institutions depend on recollection and recollection fades.

It is important to recognize that architecture does not eliminate conflict. It channels conflict productively. When disagreement arises within structured systems, resolution pathways exist. Voting thresholds determine outcomes. Mediation clauses reduce escalation. Clear authority lines prevent paralysis. Architecture turns potential fracture into managed tension.

The absence of architecture is often invisible during prosperity. Revenue growth can mask structural weakness. Strong leadership can compensate for undefined processes. Loyalty can temporarily overcome unclear roles. However, when transition or crisis occurs, the absence of architecture becomes exposed. Institutions that appeared stable can fracture quickly. Architecture reveals its value most clearly during stress.

The Aristologist measures success differently. He evaluates whether systems function independently of his constant supervision. He observes whether governance meetings proceed effectively without his direct control. He assesses whether successors can navigate complexity within documented frameworks. He views institutional resilience as the highest achievement.

There is a deeper philosophical element within this architecture. Permanence requires surrendering the illusion of centrality. The founder must accept that the institution is not an extension of his personality but an entity that must outlive him. This requires psychological maturity. It requires allowing structure to become more important than individual preference.

Examine your own architecture with honesty. Is governance documented comprehensively? Are ownership structures consolidated strategically? Is succession embedded within governance rather than treated as an afterthought. Are financial reserves sufficient to absorb volatility? Is culture written and reinforced? Are oversight mechanisms active and independent? These questions reveal whether permanence is aspiration or design.

The architecture of permanence is deliberate. It is disciplined. It is often invisible to observers yet decisive across generations. It transforms power from personal strength into institutional stability.

As this chapter closes, understand this clearly. What stands longest was designed deepest.

Build beneath the surface and what rises will endure above it.

Chapter Reflection & Strategic Notes
The Rise of the Aristologist

CHAPTER THIRTEEN

THE FOUR LAWS OF GENERATIONAL AUTHORITY

Every enduring system in history has rested upon governing laws. Empires were stabilized by codified legal frameworks. Financial systems were strengthened by principles that regulated exchange and accountability. Institutions that survived centuries did so because they operated according to consistent structural truths rather than emotional impulse. Aristology is no different. It does not rely on inspiration alone. It is anchored in laws that define how generational authority must function if permanence is to be achieved.

The Four Laws of Generational Authority are not suggestions. They are structural realities observed across centuries of rise and decline. They emerge from historical evidence and institutional analysis. They explain why some families multiply influence across generations while others dissipate strength within decades. They clarify why certain organizations endure leadership transitions without instability while others fracture under pressure. These laws operate whether acknowledged or ignored. The difference lies in whether leaders design with them or against them.

The First Law of Generational Authority is that power must be institutional before it can be intergenerational. Authority concentrated solely on an individual who cannot survive that individual. History demonstrates this repeatedly. Political regimes built around charismatic rulers collapsed when succession lacked structure. Businesses dependent entirely on founders struggled when those founders departed. Families whose wealth revolved around one central decision maker fractured when coordination disappeared. Institutionalization transforms personality into process. It transfers authority from impulse to governance. Without institutionalization, generational continuity is mathematically improbable.

Institutionalization requires documentation, councils, formalized decision rights, and defined succession frameworks. It requires that authority be embedded in charters and agreements rather than residing informally in relationships. When power becomes institutional, it becomes transferable. When it remains personal, it becomes fragile.

The Second Law of Generational Authority is that ownership must be consolidated, or it will be diluted. Expansion across generations multiplies heirs, and multiplication without consolidation weakens influence. Equity divided without structure produces fragmentation. Fragmentation produces inefficiency and conflict. Many fortunes have eroded not because assets were insufficient but because ownership lacked architectural cohesion. Consolidated structures such as holding entities, defined share classes, and voting agreements protect unity of direction even as families expand numerically. Without consolidation, generational multiplication accelerates instability.

This law is not about restricting participation. It is about preserving coherence. When ownership remains strategically organized, collective authority strengthens. When ownership disperses without governance, collective authority weakens. Dilution is not merely financial. It is directional. It diminishes strategic alignment.

The Third Law of Generational Authority is that succession must be prepared before it is required. Succession delayed until crisis becomes reactive rather than strategic. Emotional decision making replaces objective evaluation. Rivalry replaces clarity. Confidence erodes. Institutions that endure succession treat a continuous process rather than a future event. Successors are mentored early. Criteria are documented clearly. Authority is transferred gradually within governance frameworks. This preparation reduces shock at transition and preserves stability.

Ignoring this law produces predictable consequences. Abrupt transitions destabilize markets, unsettle employees, and fracture families. Prepared transitions reinforce confidence and continuity. Succession is not a ceremonial moment. It is an architectural discipline.

The Fourth Law of Generational Authority is that culture must be codified, or it will drift. Culture shapes decisions across time. Values influence risk tolerance, investment philosophy, and conflict resolution. When culture remains unwritten, it becomes vulnerable to reinterpretation. As generations pass, memory fades and identity weaken. Institutions that endure preserve culture intentionally through written doctrine, education, and ritual reinforcement. Culture becomes the compass during uncertainty.

Without codified culture, growth introduces fragmentation. Different interpretations compete. Identity erodes. With codified culture, adaptation remains aligned with foundational principles. The institution evolves without losing itself.

Together, these four laws create the framework of Aristology. Institutionalization, consolidation, preparation, and codification form the backbone of generational authority. They interact with one another. Institutionalization supports consolidation. Consolidation reinforces succession stability. Succession planning protects culture. Culture sustains institutional purpose.

The failure to respect these laws explains the recurrence of the three-generation collapse. When power remains personal, when ownership fragments, when succession is delayed, and when culture drifts, decline becomes almost inevitable. These outcomes are not mysteries. They are structural consequences.

Examine the history of multigenerational enterprises that have endured across centuries. Whether in finance, manufacturing, or philanthropy, those that survived applied these laws implicitly or explicitly. They formalized governance structures early. They consolidate equity within defined vehicles. They prepared theirs systematically. They documented values and mission clearly. Their survival was not accidental. It was architectural.

The Aristologist treats these laws as operating principles. Every strategic decision is evaluated against them. Expansion is pursued only when institutional strength can support it. Equity distribution is considered only within consolidated frameworks. Leadership development begins long before leadership transfer. Cultural reinforcement accompanies growth.

These laws also apply beyond families to corporations and communities. Organizations that institutionalize authority rather than centralize it survive leadership change. Companies that consolidate ownership strategically maintain direction. Institutions that plan succession proactively preserve market confidence. Cultural clarity prevents drift during expansion.

There is moral seriousness within these laws. Generational authority carries responsibility not only for wealth but for stability. When institutions collapse, employees suffer, communities destabilize, and opportunity diminishes. Respecting these laws protects more than private interest. It protects ecosystems of influence.

Reflect deeply on whether your current structures align with these laws. Is authority institutionalized beyond personality? Is ownership consolidated strategically? Is succession prepared before necessity? Is culture documented and reinforced? If any of these pillars are weak, permanence is uncertain.

The Four Laws of Generational Authority are not theoretical ideals. They are structural realities. They explain decline and they explain endurance.

Authority that ignores law becomes temporary. Authority that respects law becomes permanent.

Build with these laws in mind and what you construct will not depend solely on you.

Chapter Reflection & Strategic Notes
The Rise of the Aristologist

CHAPTER FOURTEEN

WEALTH THAT THINKS IN DECADES

The greatest divide between temporary prosperity and generational strength is not income level. It is time horizon. Wealth that thinks in months behaves differently than wealth that thinks in decades. Wealth that thinks in quarters chases performance metrics. Wealth that thinks in decades engineers' stability. Wealth that thinks in a single lifetime seeks accumulation. Wealth that thinks across generations seeks compounding continuity. Aristology demands a transformation from a financial perspective from immediacy to endurance.

Modern economic culture rewards speed. Quarterly earnings reports dominate decision making. Short term returns influence investor behavior. Consumer culture encourages visible consumption as proof of success. Under such conditions, capital often moves rapidly but shallowly. It seeks quick advantage. It celebrates liquidity over longevity. It prioritizes expansion over protection. This environment produces impressive gains but fragile systems.

Wealth that thinks in decades operates under different assumptions. It recognizes that economic cycles are inevitable. Booms are followed by contractions. Markets expand and correct. Industries are evolving. Technological disruption reshapes entire sectors. Therefore, capital must be positioned not merely to grow in favorable conditions but to survive adverse ones. Durability becomes as important as return.

Historically, families and institutions that endured across centuries demonstrated this long horizon mindset. Banking dynasties in Europe consolidated capital within structured entities, diversified holdings across industries and geographies, and reinvested earnings rather than extracting excessive distributions. Endowments attached to universities were managed with policies designed to preserve principal while generating sustainable yield. These models reveal that permanence requires restraint as much as ambition.

Restraint is often misunderstood as lack of confidence. In truth, it is discipline. Wealth that thinks in decades resists overleveraging for rapid scale. It avoids concentration risk that could destabilize the entire structure. It balances liquidity with strategic investment. It builds reserves to absorb downturns. It prioritizes compounding over spectacle.

Compounding is the quiet force behind generational wealth. When capital remains consolidated and reinvested consistently, it multiplies in ways that exceed short term speculation. Fragmentation disrupts compounding. Excessive distribution weakens reinvestment. Emotional spending erodes foundation. Aristology treats compounding as a strategic discipline. It encourages policies that reinvest profits into diversified, income generating assets aligned with long term mission.

Wealth that thinks in decades also integrates governance into financial strategy. Investment decisions are not made impulsively. They are evaluated within defined parameters. Risk tolerance is documented. Asset allocation policies are reviewed periodically. Independent oversight ensures accountability. Financial architecture aligns with institutional goals rather than individual preference.

Another dimension of long horizon wealth is intergenerational education. Capital can be transferred legally within days. Understanding takes years. Heirs must be taught the philosophy behind investment strategies. They must understand why reserves are maintained, why leverage is limited, why diversification matters, and why patience protects compounding. Without this education, new decision makers may pursue short term gain at the expense of long-term stability.

Time horizon also shapes lifestyle decisions. Visible consumption often signals immediate success but can undermine structural capital. Wealth that thinks in decades evaluates expenditure not solely by desire but by impact on compounding power. This does not prohibit enjoyment. It prioritizes sustainability.

Consider the difference between extracting all available profit annually and allocating a portion toward reserves and reinvestment. The former maximizes short term liquidity. The latter strengthens long term durability. When downturns occur, institutions that preserved capital withstand stress while others liquidate assets under pressure. Decade thinking prevents reactive liquidation.

Economic ecosystems further illustrate this principle. Communities supported by institutions with long horizon strategies experience stable employment and philanthropic continuity. When organizations prioritize immediate extraction over reinvestment, communities experience volatility.

Aristology recognizes that financial discipline extends beyond private wealth into public impact.

Wealth that thinks in decades also prepares for succession financially. Ownership structures are consolidated within vehicles that preserve strategic alignment. Trusts may include provisions that encourage reinvestment rather than fragmentation. Voting agreements protect long term mission. Financial transfer becomes part of architectural planning rather than a reactive distribution.

It is essential to confront a difficult truth. Short term thinking feels productive because it generates immediate results. Long term thinking requires patience and often appears slower. However, over decades, patience compounds while impulsiveness dissipates. The difference is rarely visible in the first year but becomes undeniable across generations.

Financial history is filled with examples of rapid fortune creation followed by equally rapid collapse because capital was not structured for endurance. Market bubbles illustrate this clearly. Speculative gains create illusion of permanent prosperity until volatility reveals fragility. Institutions grounded in diversified and disciplined capital allocation survive these cycles with stability.

Aristology therefore insists that wealth strategy must be integrated with governance strategy. Capital allocation decisions must align with institutional mission. Risk must be evaluated not only in financial terms but in generational terms. An investment that promises extraordinary return but threatens structural stability must be scrutinized.

Time horizon thinking also influences philanthropy. Enduring philanthropic institutions establish endowments rather than one-time distributions. Endowments preserve principal and generate sustainable impact. This model reflects Aristological discipline. It converts wealth into continuous influence rather than temporary generosity.

Examine your own financial strategy honestly. Does it prioritize visible growth over protected compounding? Are reserves adequate to absorb downturns? Are investments diversified intentionally? Are heirs educated in capital stewardship? Are ownership vehicles structured to prevent fragmentation? These questions reveal whether wealth thinks in years or in decades.

The psychological shift required for decade thinking is significant. It requires resisting cultural pressure for immediate display. It demands patience when rapid expansion appears attractive. It calls for humility in acknowledging economic uncertainty. It requires faith in compounding discipline rather than speculative excitement.

The Aristologist evaluates every financial decision with generational consequence in mind. He asks how this allocation will affect successors. He examines whether capital remains protected within structure. He prioritizes durability over dominance.

Wealth that thinks in decades does not chase applause. It builds stability. It does not seek the highest peak at any cost. It seeks the strongest foundation across time.

Temporary wealth seeks speed. Permanent wealth seeks structure.

Capital that is patient becomes powerful. Capital that is impulsive becomes fragile.

Think beyond the quarter and you will build beyond your lifetime.

Chapter Reflection & Strategic Notes
The Rise of the Aristologist

CHAPTER FIFTEEN

GOVERNANCE BEFORE GROWTH

Growth is intoxicating. It validates strategy. It signals relevance. It attracts investors, followers, customers, and admirers. When revenue increases and influence expand, leaders feel momentum beneath them. Momentum creates confidence. Confidence creates acceleration. Yet acceleration without governance is the most dangerous phase in the lifecycle of any institution. Growth exposes weakness faster than decline does. Decline reduces complexity. Growth multiplies it. If governance is not established before expansion, the very success that leaders celebrate becomes the catalyst of instability.

Governance is the discipline that defines how authority operates under complexity. It clarifies decision rights. It establishes accountability. It creates boundaries within which growth can occur safely. Without governance, growth amplifies confusion. More revenue introduces more stakeholders. More stakeholders introduce more perspectives. More perspectives without defined structure introduce conflict. Governance absorbs that complexity by converting ambiguity into process.

The mistake many founders make is postponing governance because it appears unnecessary during early success. When teams are small and decisions are centralized, informal communication feels efficient. Authority flows quickly. Adaptation is immediate. Documentation seems burdensome. However, the same informality that feels agile at small scale becomes chaotic at large scale. As organizations expand, what was once clarity becomes assumption. What was once trust becomes tension. What was once flexibility becomes inconsistency.

Governance must precede growth if growth is to remain stable. It must be constructed while complexity is manageable rather than retrofitted when pressure mounts. Leaders who establish boards, document roles, codify voting procedures, and formalize financial oversight early create foundations that can support scale. Leaders who delay governance often find themselves reacting to crises rather than guiding expansion deliberately.

History demonstrates this principle repeatedly. Corporations that scaled rapidly without strengthening internal controls often encountered financial misreporting, compliance failures, and strategic drift. Political movements that gained popularity without institutional frameworks fractured when competing factions emerged. Family enterprises that expanded geographically without defined leadership hierarchies struggled when generational transition arrived. Growth magnifies whatever exists. If structure is strong, growth multiplies stability. If structure is weak, growth multiplies instability.

Governance is often misunderstood as limitation. In truth, it is liberation. It liberates leaders from being the sole decision maker. It liberates organizations from personality dependency. It liberates stakeholders from uncertainty. Clear governance accelerates growth because it reduces friction. Decisions move efficiently within defined authority. Conflicts are resolved within documented frameworks. Strategic direction remains coherent despite expansion.

The architecture of governance includes several critical elements. Defined leadership roles prevent overlaps and rivalry. Independent oversight introduces accountability. Financial controls protect assets from mismanagement. Risk management protocols anticipate volatility. Succession plans ensure continuity. These components operate together as stabilizers beneath visible growth.

Consider the analogy of structural engineering. A building designed to support additional floors requires foundational reinforcement before expansion. Adding floors without reinforcing the base invites collapse. In the same way, adding markets, products, employees, or heirs without reinforcing governance invites fragility. Growth must be supported proportionally by structure.

There is also a psychological dimension to governance before growth. Leaders must resist the ego satisfaction of rapid expansion when structural readiness is insufficient. This requires humility. It requires acknowledging that governance is not a bureaucratic inconvenience but a strategic necessity. It demands patience when opportunities appear attractive, but governance frameworks remain immature.

Governance also protects culture during growth. As organizations expand, new members bring diverse perspectives. Without documented values and behavioral expectations, identity can drift. Governance embeds culture into policy and practice. It ensures that growth does not dilute mission.

Financial governance deserves particular emphasis. Rapid revenue increases can mask weaknesses in accounting, capital allocation, and risk assessment. Leaders intoxicated by growth may overlook warning signals. Independent financial oversight, periodic audits, and disciplined reporting systems prevent expansion from becoming reckless. Financial transparency strengthens confidence among stakeholders and reduces vulnerability during downturns.

Growth without governance often centralizes authority further because leaders feel compelled to control expanding complexity personally. This creates bottlenecks and exhaustion. Governance distributes responsibility within defined boundaries. It multiplies capacity while maintaining coherence.

Examine your own trajectory. Has expansion outpaced governance. Are decision rights clearly documented? Does oversight operate independently? Are financial controls rigorous? Is succession integrated into governance structures? If any of these areas remain informal while growth accelerates, instability is accumulating quietly.

The Aristologist evaluates opportunity not solely by potential revenue but by structural readiness. He asks whether governance can absorb increased complexity. He strengthens oversight before entering new markets. He refines role clarity before adding leadership layers. He ensures that ownership structures remain consolidated during expansion. Growth is welcomed, but only when structure is prepared.

The most devastating collapses in business history often occurred not during stagnation but after explosive growth. Overextension, compliance failures, cultural drift, and leadership conflict frequently followed periods of rapid expansion. These collapses were rarely caused by lack of ambition. They were caused by lack of governance.

Governance before growth also stabilizes generational transfer. When institutions grow without formalized decision-making processes, successors inherit confusion. When governance is strong, successors inherit clarity. Growth then becomes opportunity rather than burden.

The discipline of governance does not eliminate risk. It mitigates it. It does not slow innovation. It stabilizes it. It does not suppress ambition. It channels it responsibly.

As leaders reflect on their journey, they must ask whether their structures are built to support the level of expansion they pursue. If not, the pursuit must pause until architecture strengthens. True strength is not measured by how fast one grows but by how securely one grows.

Temporary expansion impresses observers. Structured expansion endures across generations.

Build the framework before you multiply the floors.

Governance is not the enemy of growth. It is the guardian of it.

Grow only as fast as your structure can sustain.

Chapter Reflection & Strategic Notes
The Rise of the Aristologist

CHAPTER SIXTEEN

THE FAMILY AS AN INSTITUTION

I learned how to build infrastructure in the marketplace before I fully understood that I had to build infrastructure inside my own bloodline. In business, the lesson was clear. If I did not control the channel, I would always depend on someone who did. Shelf space was not merely placement in a liquor store. It was leverage. Distribution agreements were not paperwork. They were powerful. Direct to consumers was not a marketing strategy. It was ownership of relationship. Media platforms were not vanity projects. They were narrative control. When I decided to build my own channel, it was because I recognized that authority does not come from participating alone. Authority comes from infrastructure. Infrastructure determines who moves freely and who waits for permission.

As I built brands and expanded into regulated industries, I came to understand that product excellence without distribution is vulnerability. You can have the finest bottle, the strongest message, the most compelling story, but if someone else controls access to the customer, they shape your destiny. That realization changed how I built. I stopped thinking only in terms of sales and started thinking in terms of systems. I focused on access, control, consolidation, and permanence. I wanted to own the pipeline between what I created and the world that consumed it.

But there came a moment when I recognized something deeper. If I was disciplined enough to engineer infrastructure externally, I had to be disciplined enough to engineer it internally. If my family was the ultimate owner of brands, intellectual property, distribution relationships, and audience channels, then my family could not remain informal. The moment assets move through a bloodline, that bloodline becomes an institution whether it chooses to acknowledge it or not. Institutions without governance fracture under pressure. Institutions without documentation drift under complexity. Institutions without role clarity collapse during transition.

I did not raise my children to seek employment alone. I raised them to create. Every one of my children was raised with entrepreneurial thinking as a baseline, not an option. I wanted them to understand ownership before comfort. I wanted them to see opportunity where others saw obstacles. I wanted them to build channels instead of standing in line. That was not accidental parenting. That was cultural architecture.

Each of my children carries a distinct quality and a unique set of characteristics. They do not think alike. They do not approach problems the same way. One may carry creative fire and visionary instinct. One may move with strategic precision and analytical discipline. One may embody operational steadiness and long-range focus. None of them are copies of mine, and none of them are copies of each other. I never intended to be uniform. I intended strength.

What unites them is not personality. It is the power to create. That power was cultivated intentionally. It was modeled on how I built businesses, wrote books, negotiated agreements, created brands, and refused dependency. They watched structure being built. They watched channels being secured.

They watched authority being claimed through infrastructure rather than granted by permission.

However, individual entrepreneurial power is not the same as generational permanence. Talent alone does not create alignment. Creativity alone does not produce coordination. Independence alone does not ensure unity. If left unstructured, strong personalities can move in separate directions. If left undocumented, shared assets can become points of tension. If left undefined, roles can blur and expectations can clash.

If I believe in channel ownership in the marketplace, then I must believe in structural alignment in my household. The same discipline I apply to distribution contracts must apply to family governance. The same clarity I demand in brand positioning must exist in role definition. The same seriousness I apply to compliance in regulated industries must exist in succession planning within my bloodline.

I do not want a collection of independent entrepreneurs connected only by last name. I want a coordinated generational institution anchored in shared doctrine, consolidated ownership, and documented governance. I want their individual strengths to compound rather than compete. I want differences to harmonize rather than fragment. That does not happen by emotion alone. It happens by design.

Family must be structured with the same intensity as business. That means documented ownership consolidation. That means clarity between compensation for operational roles and equity for generational stake. That means written expectations for participation. That means a constitution that outlines mission, values, voting structures, dispute resolution mechanisms, and succession criteria. That means formal education in the regulatory complexity of spirits distribution, the economics of brand leverage, the mechanics of direct-to-consumer infrastructure, and the discipline of capital preservation.

If I built infrastructure externally but neglected infrastructure internally, I would undermine my own philosophy. Building the channel externally was about eliminating dependency. Building governance internally is about eliminating fragmentation. Both are forms of permanence.

My children were raised to create, but they must also be aligned to construct collectively. Individually they can build ventures. Collectively, under documented structure, they can build legacy. Without architecture, even powerful creators can drift apart over time. With architecture, they become coordinated force.

I refuse to assume unity will survive complexity without governance. I refuse to postpone documentation because harmony exists today. I understand that complexity multiplies over time, not decreases. Assets grow. Visibility increases. Influence expands. Pressure follows. If governance is weak, pressure exposes fracture. If governance is strong, pressure strengthens cohesion.

The brands I built, the books I wrote, the platforms I created, the audiences I cultivated, and the distribution channels I secured are not temporary ventures. They are generational assets. Intellectual property carries value. Audience relationships carry leverage. Shelf space carries power. Direct pipelines carry control. These must be consolidated within defined structures so that they are not diluted by ambiguity during transition.

My responsibility is not only to create wealth. It is to design continuity. It is to ensure that when my presence diminishes, the structure remains intact. It is to ensure that each child understands not only what we own but how it functions, why it was structured the way it was, and how it must be preserved.

When their individual qualities operate within governance, something larger emerges. They simply do not remain entrepreneurs. They become institutional architects. They move from isolated creation to coordinated construction.

The family must function as an institution because it carries institutional weight. It must have councils. It must have recorded minutes. It must have financial review sessions. It must have documented voting protocols. It must have defined succession criteria. It must distinguish operational leadership from ownership rights clearly.

This is not cold detachment. It is disciplined love. It is protection of unity. It is insulation against unnecessary conflict. It is respectful for what has been built.

Infrastructure in the marketplace created leverage. Infrastructure in the family creates longevity. If I own distribution externally, I must own alignment internally. If I control channels in commerce, I must control governance in bloodline.

My children were raised with the power to create. When those powers are structured, aligned, and governed intentionally, they will become more than individual entrepreneurs. They will become a coordinated generational institution.

Creation opens opportunity. Structure preserves it. Coordination multiplies it.

Chapter Reflection & Strategic Notes
The Rise of the Aristologist

CHAPTER SEVENTEEN

THE HOLDING COMPANY MINDSET

Most entrepreneurs build businesses. Very few build structures that can hold businesses together across generations. There is a significant difference between operating a successful brand and architecting an ecosystem that survives complexity, expansion, and transition. The holding company mindset is the difference between ownership and consolidation, between activity and architecture, between revenue and permanence.

A holding company is not merely a legal entity. It is a philosophy of control. It is the deliberate decision to separate operations from ownership while consolidating authority at the structural level. It recognizes that brands may rise and fall, products may evolve, markets may shift, but consolidated control preserves direction. The holding company mindset asks a foundational question that most founders never consider deeply enough. Who truly owns the engine behind all of this?

When I built brands and distribution channels, I was not simply creating products. I was creating leverage. I was creating relationships with retailers, restaurants, regulators, media platforms, and consumers. Each agreement added complexity. Each brand added moving parts. Each new channel added operational weight. Over time I understood that without consolidation, complexity can become fragmented. When assets exist in isolation, they are vulnerable. When they exist under unified structure, they compound.

The holding company mindset begins with clarity of ownership. Instead of allowing each brand to operate as an isolated island, the structure consolidates intellectual property, equity interests, and strategic control under a centralized umbrella. This umbrella does not suffocate creativity. It stabilizes it. It ensures that strategic direction remains cohesive even as individual ventures evolve.

There is a psychological shift that must occur for a founder to embrace this mindset. Entrepreneurs often identify deeply with specific brands. The brand becomes personal. The logo becomes symbolic. The market response becomes emotional. The holding company mindset requires stepping back from emotional attachment to individual ventures and asking whether the structure beneath them is designed to endure. It requires recognizing that brands are expressions of a larger institutional engine.

When multiple brands exist within a family ecosystem, governance must rise above operational noise. The holding company structure allows operational teams to focus on execution while strategic authority remains consolidated. This reduces internal competition and clarifies decision making. It defines who allocates capital. It defines who approves expansion. It defines how profits are reinvested. Without this clarity, growth introduces rivalry.

Another core advantage of holding the company mindset is risk insulation. When assets are layered properly, liability in one operational entity does not automatically destabilize the entire ecosystem. This structural separation protects generational capital. It prevents a single setback from triggering systemic collapse. Entrepreneurs who operate without this insulation often discover too late that vulnerability was built into their structure.

The holding company mindset also strengthens negotiation power. When partners understand that they are engaging with a consolidated institution rather than a fragmented set of ventures, perception shifts. Authority increases. Credibility strengthens. Scale becomes visible. Consolidation signals seriousness.

Within a family context, the holding company mindset creates generational alignment. Instead of dividing ownership across scattered entities without coordination, equity can be centralized strategically. Voting rights can be structured intentionally. Succession can be integrated at the holding level rather than renegotiated across individual brands. This prevents dilution of influence as generations expand.

I understand that building direct to consumer channels was an act of control. I refused to depend solely on traditional distribution because dependency weakens leverage. The holding company mindset extends that logic further. It ensures that the ownership of those channels is consolidated under disciplined governance. Owning the pipeline is powerful. Structuring ownership of the pipeline is permanent.

It is also important to understand that consolidation does not mean rigidity. The holding company mindset encourages entrepreneurial experimentation at the operational level. New brands can be launched. Markets can be tested. Strategies can evolve. But beneath that activity lies stable architecture. The foundation does not move every time a product changes.

Generational wealth is often destroyed by fragmentation rather than failure. When ownership divides informally among heirs, strategic alignment weakens. When operational leadership conflicts with ownership expectations, tension increases. The holding company structure separates these issues. Ownership resides within defined vehicles. Operational leadership is appointed based on competence. Governance oversees both.

There is also a capital allocation discipline embedded within this mindset. Profits from successful brands can be reinvested strategically across the ecosystem. Underperforming ventures can be evaluated objectively without emotional collapse. The institution becomes resilient because it operates as a portfolio rather than a single bet.

The holding company mindset requires documented governance at the top. Boards or councils review performance across entities. Financial reporting consolidates data for strategic visibility. Succession planning is embedded at the consolidated level. Intellectual property rights are centralized rather than scattered. This clarity strengthens both internal unity and external credibility.

When families fail to adopt this mindset, generational expansion complicates everything. Each heir may hold partial stakes in separate ventures. Disagreements over direction escalate. Liquidity pressures introduce forced sales. Emotional disputes spill into operational decisions. Fragmentation accelerates erosion.

When families adopt this mindset, expansion becomes structured. Equity is centralized within defined agreements. Voting thresholds are clear. Dispute resolution processes are documented. Compensation policies distinguish operational contribution from ownership entitlement. Education prepares heirs to understand the structure rather than inherit confusion.

The holding company mindset is not about control for ego. It is about control for continuity. It acknowledges that complexity will increase over time and prepares architecture to absorb it. It treats growth not as chaos but as layered design.

Examine the structure honestly. Are intellectual property rights consolidated or scattered? Are brand equities layered under unified ownership or isolated? Are succession plans integrated at the top level? Is capital allocation coordinated or reactive? Are heirs prepared to understand the architecture they will inherit? These questions determine whether the ecosystem will multiply or fragment.

There is power in consolidation. There is stability in layered ownership. There is leverage in unified governance. When the holding company mindset is embraced fully, brands become components of a larger institution rather than isolated achievements.

Entrepreneurs build businesses. Architects build systems that hold businesses.

Ownership is powerful. Consolidated ownership is enduring.

Structure the engine, not just the vehicle.

Chapter Reflection & Strategic Notes
The Rise of the Aristologist

CHAPTER EIGHTEEN

PROTECTING THE CROWN THROUGH STRUCTURE

The Rise of the Aristologist is not the story of acquiring power. It is the discipline of preserving it. History is filled with men and women who rose rapidly, commanded markets, shaped culture, accumulated influence, and then disappeared within a generation because the crown they earned was never structurally protected. The public often confuses visibility with permanence, but permanence is never guaranteed by applause. It is guaranteed by architecture. The Aristologist does not ask how high he can rise. He asks how long what he builds will remain standing after he is no longer there to hold it together.

The crown is a metaphor, but it is also a warning. In every era, those who achieved dominance faced the same hidden challenge. Once authority is consolidated, it must be shielded from erosion. Erosion rarely arrives through dramatic defeat. It arrives quietly through dilution of ownership, undefined succession, fragmented governance, and emotional decision making. The visible empire can appear stable while its structural foundation is weakening beneath it.

Consider the history of monarchies. Empires that expanded

through conquest often collapsed not because of foreign invasion but because succession was unclear. When rulers failed to document transition, rival factions emerged. Brothers turned against brothers. Generals split allegiances. Advisors formed camps. The crown, once a symbol of unity, became the object of internal fracture. The failure was not ambition. It was architecture.

The same pattern exists in modern commerce. Founders build companies from nothing into powerful institutions, only to watch them destabilize during leadership transition. When ownership is dispersed loosely among heirs without voting agreements, paralysis sets in. When governance is informal, disputes escalate into division. When intellectual property rights are not centralized, assets are licensed, sold, or diluted without strategic alignment. Competitors do not take the crown. It is weakened internally.

The Rise of the Aristologist demands that we confront this pattern honestly. If the goal is to architect power that outlives you, then protecting the crown must become deliberate. Protection is not defensive to fear. It is structural intelligence.

When I chose to build my own channel rather than rely entirely on traditional gatekeepers, I was engaging in crown protection at the commercial level. I understood that if distribution is controlled externally, influence can be withdrawn at any moment. If retailers decide to replace you, your market access disappears. If platforms change algorithms, your audience vanishes. Owning infrastructure protects authority. Direct to consumer pipelines, consolidated media platforms, and structured brand ownership are shields against dependency.

However, commercial infrastructure alone is insufficient. The deeper crown is ownership itself. Intellectual property, equity in brands, distribution agreements, contracts, and audience relationships are assets that must be layered intentionally. If these are scattered across informal arrangements, they become vulnerable during generational transfer. If they are consolidated under structured entities with documented governance, they become fortified.

The Aristologist sees consolidation as insulation. He understands that separating operational entities while centralizing strategic ownership prevents single points of failure. In history, powerful merchant families in Europe built layered ownership structures precisely for this reason. Their trading houses operated independently across regions, but strategic control remained centralized through family councils and consolidated equity. When one region suffered an economic downturn, the entire enterprise did not collapse. Risk was distributed. Authority remained unified.

Modern corporate conglomerates operate on similar principles. Holding companies own diverse subsidiaries across industries. The purpose is not merely diversification. It is controlled at scale. Operational management may vary, but strategic direction remains anchored at the top. This layered architecture allows growth without surrendering authority.

The future will reward those who understand this even more clearly. Markets are becoming more volatile. Technology accelerates disruption. Consumer loyalty shifts rapidly. Regulatory environments evolve. In such conditions, only institutions with structural resilience will endure. Personal brands without consolidated ownership will fade. Businesses built around charisma without governance will fracture. Families that inherit complexity without documentation will struggle.

Protecting the crown also requires psychological discipline.

Founders often struggle to transfer authority because identity becomes fused with control. The Aristologist recognizes that embedding authority into structure is not loss. It is legacy. When governance documents clarify decision rights and succession protocols, they do not weaken the founder's impact. They extend it.

Consider the difference between a leader who personally approves every decision and a leader who builds systems that operate effectively without constant intervention. The first model creates dependency. The second model creates permanence. The crown is not protected by personal dominance. It is protected by institutional design.

There is also a moral dimension to protecting the crown. When institutions collapse due to poor structure, employees lose stability, partners lose confidence, and communities lose support. Protecting authority through architecture safeguards more than personal wealth. It protects ecosystems of influence.

In my own journey, the lesson became clear. Building brands was necessary. Securing distribution was strategic. Writing doctrine was powerful. But without consolidating ownership and documenting governance across generations, all of it could become temporary. The rise means nothing if decline follows immediately after transition.

The Aristologist studies decline as carefully as he studies success. He asks what caused erosion in other dynasties. He observes how fragmentation weakened influence. He learns from corporate collapses where founders postponed succession planning. He analyzes how families lost leverage when equity was divided impulsively.

Protecting the crown requires four deliberate commitments. Consolidate ownership. Document governance. Formalize succession. Educate heirs. These commitments operate together as structural armor.

Consolidation ensures that authority is not diluted across uncontrolled entities. Governance defines how decisions are made and how disputes are resolved. Succession planning removes ambiguity at transition. Education prepares the next generation to steward what they inherit responsibly.

The Rise of the Aristologist is incomplete without this discipline. Power without protection is temporary. Authority without architecture is fragile. Influence without insulation is vulnerable.

The crown is not the product. It is not the logo. It is not applause. The crown is the structured control of infrastructure, equity, and direction. If that structure is weak, the crown slips.

History has proven this repeatedly. The future will prove it again.

The Aristologist does not rise for the moment. He rises to remain.

Protect the crown through structure, and the authority you build will not fade with you.

Chapter Reflection & Strategic Notes
The Rise of the Aristologist

CHAPTER NINETEEN

BUILDING ECONOMIC ECOSYSTEMS THAT MULTIPLY

Permanent power is never built on a single revenue stream. It is never dependent on a single product. It is never vulnerable to a single market condition. Aristology teaches that authority becomes durable when it evolves from an isolated enterprise into a coordinated ecosystem. An ecosystem is not a collection of businesses. It is a structured network of mutually reinforcing assets designed to multiply with one another rather than compete for survival.

The Doctrine of Permanent Power requires multiplication, not expansion for its own sake, but intentional compounding across interconnected platforms. Expansion without ecosystem thinking produces scattered ventures. Ecosystem architecture produces leverage. The difference lies in whether each new initiative strengthens the whole or operates independently from it.

History reveals that the most enduring institutions understood this principle long before modern terminology described it. Merchant dynasties did not rely solely on trade. They integrated shipping, banking, warehousing, and political relationships. Industrial magnates did not operate only factories. They controlled rail transport, steel production, distribution hubs, and financial backing. Universities built endowments, research arms, publishing houses, and alumni networks that reinforced one another. In each case, power multiplied because assets were integrated rather than isolated.

The Aristologist builds economic ecosystems deliberately. He asks how each venture supports the others. He designs vertical alignment, where production, distribution, and consumer access operate within controlled pathways. He designs horizontal reinforcement, where media, intellectual property, education, and commerce amplify one another. Each component feeds the next.

In your own journey, building brands was not an isolated act. Creating distribution channels strengthened brand leverage. Publishing doctrine strengthened authority. Media appearances reinforce credibility. Live events-built community loyalty. Direct to consumer systems created data ownership. Each layer reinforced the others. This is ecosystem thinking in motion.

An ecosystem multiplies because it reduces friction. When one branch of the system introduces a consumer to the brand, another branch deepens engagement. When intellectual property educates an audience, product lines provide tangible participation. When community platforms gather supporters, distribution pipelines convert interest into transaction. No single component operates alone. The architecture ensures flow.

The Doctrine of Permanent Power requires this integration because isolated success is fragile. A single product may decline. A single platform may change algorithms. A single market may contract. An ecosystem absorbs volatility because its components stabilize one another.

Economic ecosystems also strengthen generational transition. Heirs inheriting a diversified and interconnected structure face opportunity rather than confusion. When governance documents clarify how each entity relates to the others, strategic direction remains intact. When ownership is centralized at the holding level, ecosystem alignment persists even as operational leadership evolves.

Another critical dimension of ecosystem building is narrative consistency. Authority multiplies when messaging across brands and platforms reinforces a unified philosophy. The doctrine behind your books strengthens the philosophy behind your brands. The philosophy behind your brands strengthens the credibility of your events. The credibility of your events strengthens your distribution leverage. This is narrative compounding.

Ecosystems also allow capital recycling. Profits from one sector can fund innovation in another. Mature ventures can stabilize emerging initiatives. Risk is distributed intelligently rather than concentrated recklessly. This is how institutions endure technological disruption and economic cycles.

Looking toward the future, economic ecosystems will become even more critical. Digital platforms will continue to fragment attention. Regulatory frameworks will evolve. Consumer trust will shift toward institutions that demonstrate coherence and authenticity. Those who operate isolated ventures will struggle to maintain consistency. Those who build integrated systems will command influence.

The Aristologist understands that multiplication is not chaos. It is coordination. He resists launching ventures that do not align strategically with the ecosystem. He evaluates whether new initiatives strengthen existing infrastructure or distract from it. Discipline governs expansion.

Economic ecosystems also expand beyond commerce into community. When brands, education, media, and events converge, a loyal base forms. That base becomes both consumer and advocate. Authority deepens. Influence extends beyond transaction into culture. Culture strengthens permanence.

The rise described in this book is not about singular success stories. It is about systemic authority. Architecting power that outlives you requires constructing environments where compounds organically influence compounds. Ecosystems achieve what individual ventures cannot. They create self-reinforcing momentum.

Examine the current structure honestly. Are your ventures integrated strategically or operating in parallel isolation? Does each initiative strengthen the others? Is governance aligned at the top? Is ownership consolidated? Is capital allocated across the system intentionally. If these elements are fragmented, multiplication will stall.

Ecosystems require design. They require periodic review. They require discipline in pruning distractions. They require long-term vision beyond immediate revenue.

Temporary power scales vertically and collapses quickly. Permanent power expands structurally and stabilizes deeply.

An ecosystem does not chase growth. It compounds it.

The Aristologist does not build businesses. He builds environments where businesses reinforce one another.

Multiply through structure and your authority will not depend on a single pillar.

Architect the ecosystem and power will expand beyond your lifetime.

Chapter Reflection & Strategic Notes
The Rise of the Aristologist

CHAPTER TWENTY

DESIGNING WHAT CANNOT BE ERASED

Power can be challenged. Wealth can be spent. Influence can fade. Visibility can shift. Markets can collapse. Governments can change. Technology can disrupt entire industries within a decade. History has proven repeatedly that nothing built on surface conditions alone survives untouched. The Aristologist understands this deeply. If power is to outlive the person who built it, it must be designed in such a way that it cannot be erased.

Erasure does not always happen dramatically. It often happens quietly. A family business that thrived for forty years dissolves within one generation because governance was never documented. A powerful brand fades because intellectual property was not consolidated. A once respected institution fractured because succession was postponed. The erosion is gradual, but the outcome is permanent. What once stood strong becomes a memory.

Designing what cannot be erased requires a different level of thinking. It requires stepping beyond immediate results and asking a more difficult question. If I disappear tomorrow, does the structure remain intact? If leadership changes, does direction remain clear. If conflict emerges, is there a documented path for resolution? If opportunity expands, is their architecture strong enough to absorb it?

The Doctrine of Permanent Power rests on this premise. Authority that is not embedded in structure will eventually dissolve. The Aristologist refuses to rely on personality alone. He embeds philosophy into governance. He embeds ownership into layered entities. He embeds culture into written doctrine. He embeds succession into documented processes. He embeds intellectual property into consolidated control.

Consider the institutions that have endured for centuries. Universities that have survived wars, economic depressions, political revolutions, and technological transformation did not survive because of charismatic presidents. They survived because charters were written. Endowments were structured. Governance bodies were formalized. Cultural values were preserved intentionally. The individuals changed. The institution remained.

The same is true for enduring corporations and family enterprises that survived multiple economic cycles. Their resilience was not accidental. It was structural. They understood that designing permanence required separation between operational activity and ownership control. It required capital discipline. It required education of heirs. It required formal oversight.

Designing what cannot be erased also requires intellectual humility. The founder must accept that he cannot personally manage every future complexity. He must trust architecture over impulse. He must design systems that function beyond his immediate oversight. This is not surrender. It is multiplication of control through structure.

In my own journey, building brands and channels was necessary, but it was not sufficient. Publishing doctrine was powerful, but it was not permanent without consolidation. Raising entrepreneurial children was important, but it was not secure without governance. The realization became clear. Creation is the beginning. Design is the safeguard.

What cannot be erased is not the logo on a bottle or the title on a book cover. What cannot be erased is consolidated ownership anchored in documented governance. What cannot be erased is a family constitution that clarifies mission and authority. What cannot be erased is intellectual property structured inside protective entities. What cannot be erased is a holding framework that aligns all ventures under unified strategy.

Technology will evolve. Markets will transform. Platforms will rise and fall. But architecture outlasts trends.

The Aristologist designs at three levels simultaneously. He designs legally through entity structure and ownership agreements. He designs culturally through doctrine, education, and values. He designs strategically through ecosystem integration and capital allocation discipline. When these layers align, erasure becomes unlikely.

There is also a generational dimension to permanence. Heirs must not only inherit assets but internalize philosophy. If doctrine is not taught, it weakens. If governance is not practiced, it decays. Designing what cannot be erased requires repetition, education, and intentional transfer of mindset.

The three-generation collapse is not fate. It is failure to design permanence. When philosophy is undocumented, heirs reinterpret. When ownership is fragmented, influence weakens. When governance is informal, conflict escalates. Designing permanence interrupts this cycle.

I look forward to fifty years. Imagine leadership transition twice over. Imagine market disruption that reshapes distribution channels entirely. Imagine regulatory changes that challenge existing structures. The question remains the same. Will the architecture absorb these shocks? If yes, the institution survives. If not, it fragments.

Designing what cannot be erased is not about immortality of ego. It is about continuity of structure. It is about ensuring that the labor of one lifetime becomes the foundation for the next rather than a temporary peak followed by decline.

This chapter closes the doctrine because Aristology is complete when permanence is engineered deliberately. The Four Laws established the framework. Governance defined authority. Wealth discipline protected capital. The family became institutional. The holding company consolidated structure. The crown was protected. The ecosystem has multiplied influences. Now permanence is sealed.

Power that depends on one voice fades when that voice is silent. Power that depends on structure remains when the voice is gone. Design deeply. Consolidate wisely. Govern clearly. Educate continuously. Multiply intentionally. When authority is architected correctly, it cannot be erased. It can evolve. It can adapt. It can grow. But it will not disappear.

This is the doctrine.

This is Aristology.

This is how power outlives you.

Chapter Reflection & Strategic Notes
The Rise of the Aristologist

CHAPTER TWENTY ONE

THE GENERATION THAT WILL NOT START OVER

History has repeated a quiet tragedy across centuries. One generation rises through sacrifice, discipline, and relentless creation. The next generation enjoys stability but must defend it. By the third generation, structure weakens, philosophy fades, and momentum dissolves. The cycle restarts. Wealth is rebuilt. Influence is regained. Authority is reconstructed. The pattern continues because permanence was never embedded deeply enough to interrupt it.

The Rise of the Aristologist was never meant to stop at structure alone. Structure without disciplined successors is vulnerable. Doctrine without embodiment becomes academic. Governance without character becomes mechanical. The final evolution of permanent power requires a new type of inheritor. A generation that does not simply receive advantage but understands architecture. A generation that does not begin from zero because systems were designed to prevent collapse. A generation that refuses to restart the climb because the foundation beneath them remains intact.

The New Aristocrat is not defined by inherited wealth. He is defined by inherited responsibility. He does not see ownership as privilege alone. He sees it as stewardship. He does not measure success by consumption. He measures it by preservation and multiplication. He does not dismantle structure for comfort. He strengthens it for continuity.

Throughout history, aristocracy was often associated with birthright and title. Authority was assumed rather than earned. The New Aristocrat rejects entitlement without discipline. He understands that inheritance without understanding leads to erosion. He recognizes that structural power must be studied, respected, and maintained. Its advantage is not comfort. His advantage is clarity.

The generation that will not start over must be educated intentionally. They must understand governance frameworks, capital allocation principles, ownership consolidation, and ecosystem integration. They must know why equity is layered under holding structures. They must understand why distribution channels were secured. They must grasp why intellectual property was centralized. They must internalize the philosophy behind Aristology so that decisions align with doctrine rather than impulse.

This generation must also be psychologically prepared. Stability can produce complacency. Comfort can weaken urgency. Visibility can inflate ego. The New Aristocrat resists these traps. He recognizes that structure does not remove responsibility. It magnifies it. When systems exist, expectations rise.

The generation that will not start over must think in decades naturally. They must instinctively evaluate whether decisions strengthen or weaken architecture. They must view capital as fuel for ecosystem expansion rather than personal display. They must treat governance meetings as sacred stewardship rather than administrative inconvenience.

The New Aristocrat also understands community responsibility. Institutions do not exist in isolation. When generational stability exists, employees gain security. Partners gain consistency. Communities gain continuity. The preservation of structure is not selfish ambition. It is social contribution.

There is a deeper transformation occurring here. The Aristologist designed permanence. The New Aristocrat embodies it. He moves with confidence not because he controls everything personally, but because he trusts the architecture beneath him. He operates within governance rather than above it. He strengthens councils rather than bypassing them. He respects voting protocols rather than manipulating them.

The generation that will not start over understands the cost of fragmentation. They study history not as distant narrative but as warning. They see how fortunes were divided because structure was weak. They see how institutions collapsed because succession was delayed. They see how ego destroyed alignment. They learn from these lessons rather than repeating them.

This generation also recognizes innovation as responsibility. Permanence does not mean stagnation. It means adaptation within architecture. The New Aristocrat does not preserve systems rigidly. He evolves them strategically. He upgrades technology. He expands ecosystems. He diversifies markets. But he does so within governance and consolidated ownership.

He is disciplined with capital. He is patient with growth. He is decisive in crisis. He is humble in prosperity. He is relentless in protecting the crown.

The Rise of the Aristologist was about designing power that outlives you. The New Aristocrat is the proof that it worked.

When governance functions without chaos, when ownership remains consolidated, when succession transitions smoothly, when ecosystem assets reinforce one another, when intellectual property remains centralized, when heirs speak the same doctrine fluently, the cycle of restart is broken.

The generation that will not start over does not begin at the bottom. They begin at structure. They begin with systems already engineered. They begin with doctrine already written. They begin with capital already consolidated. Their responsibility is not to rebuild what collapsed. Their responsibility is to elevate what endures.

The tragedy of repeated collapse becomes the testimony of intentional design.

This is not arrogance. It is preparation. It is respect for the work that came before and responsibility for the work that will follow.

The New Aristocrat does not ask what he inherited. He asks what he must protect. He does not ask what he can spend. He asks what he must strengthen. He does not ask how he can be seen. He asks how the institution can endure.

The generation that will not start over understands that starting over is expensive. It costs time, momentum, trust, and opportunity. Permanence eliminates unnecessary rebuilding. It frees energy for multiplication rather than recovery. Section II built the doctrine. Section III builds the identity capable of sustaining it. The New Aristocrat stands not on personality but on architecture. Not on inheritance alone but on understanding. Not on consumption but on stewardship.

He rises because structure supports him.

He remains because doctrine guides him.

He multiplies because ecosystem design empowers him.

The Rise of the Aristologist is complete only when the next generation does not begin from scratch.

They begin with strength.

Chapter Reflection & Strategic Notes
The Rise of the Aristologist

CHAPTER TWENTY TWO

BEYOND THE ARISTOCRAT

For centuries, the word aristocrat has carried weight. It has suggested refinement, status, privilege, influence, and inherited access to power. It has evoked images of estates, titles, political alliances, and social hierarchy. In many societies, aristocracy implied authority secured by birth rather than engineered by discipline. Influence was assumed. Wealth was inherited. Position was protected by lineage rather than structure. Yet history has demonstrated repeatedly that inherited status without architectural discipline dissolves under pressure. Titles without governance weaken. Wealth without consolidation fragments. Privilege without philosophy collapses when complexity increases. The Rise of the Aristologist demands that we move beyond the traditional understanding of aristocracy and redefine what enduring authority truly means in the modern world.

The Old Aristocrat possessed power, but he often did not understand the structural mechanics that sustained it. The New Aristocrat understands that power must be engineered intentionally. The Old Aristocrat inherited authority and relied on tradition to preserve it. The New Aristocrat inherits responsibility and relies on doctrine, governance, and disciplined architecture to protect it. The Old Aristocrat depended on lineage alone. The New Aristocrat depends on consolidated ownership, layered systems, codified philosophy, and strategic foresight. This evolution is not cosmetic. It is foundational. It separates symbolic status from structural permanence.

Historically, many aristocratic families rose through land ownership, political alliances, or military dominance. Their authority was visible, centralized, and reinforced by social order. However, as economic systems evolved from land based wealth to industrial production, then to financial capital, intellectual property, and digital infrastructure, many traditional aristocracies declined. They failed not because they lacked resources, but because they lacked adaptation within structure. They clung to symbols while neglecting systems. They guarded titles while ignoring consolidation. They protected image while allowing architecture to weaken. When markets shifted and political landscapes changed, their authority eroded because permanence had not been engineered deeply enough.

The New Aristocrat rejects symbolic security. He understands that in the modern age, land is not the only asset, and titles are not the ultimate currency. Infrastructure now includes distribution channels, intellectual property rights, brand equity, data ownership, direct consumer relationships, capital allocation strategy, and governance frameworks that operate beyond personality. Authority today is embedded in systems. It is layered across entities. It is codified in agreements. It is reinforced through disciplined oversight. To go beyond the aristocrat is to understand that nobility in the modern age is not about inherited comfort but about inherited clarity and structured responsibility.

This transformation also requires transcending ego. Traditional aristocracy often revolved around prestige and social dominance. The New Aristocrat revolves around permanence and stewardship. Prestige is fragile because it depends on perception, and perception shifts with culture and public opinion. Permanence is resilient because it depends on structure. Prestige seeks visibility. Permanence seeks durability. Prestige can be inflated quickly and deflated just as rapidly. Permanence is built slowly and reinforced deliberately. The Aristologist designs permanence so thoroughly that leadership transition does not destabilize the institution, and market volatility does not erode its foundation.

The Doctrine of Permanent Power prepared this generation for elevation. Governance was defined. Ownership was consolidated. Ecosystems were integrated. Succession was formalized. Intellectual property was centralized. Capital discipline was embedded. Now the individual must embody what the structure protects. The New Aristocrat does not measure himself by lifestyle, display, or external validation. He measures himself by alignment with doctrine and architecture. He evaluates decisions based on whether they strengthen the holding structure or weaken it. He allocates capital based on long-term compounding rather than short term gratification. He treats governance not as restriction but as reinforcement.

This mindset demands maturity. It demands resisting the temptation to dismantle structure in pursuit of personal preference. It demands recognizing that authority without accountability is instability waiting to surface. It demands honoring voting thresholds, respecting councils, maintaining documentation, and preparing successors intentionally. Entitlement weakens discipline. The New Aristocrat understands that inheritance is not proof of superiority. It is proof of obligation. It requires competence, education, and character equal to the structure inherited.

History provides clear warning. Dynasties that relied on entitlement without governance eventually faced fragmentation. Heirs disconnected from operational realities misallocated capital, liquidated strategic assets, or diluted equity through poorly structured partnerships. Without doctrine to anchor decisions, wealth eroded across generations. Without consolidation to protect control, influence dispersed. The pattern is not mysterious. It is architectural. When structure is neglected, decline accelerates.

In contrast, modern institutions that endured through industrial revolutions, technological transformation, and global economic shifts embraced adaptation within structure. They diversified holdings strategically. They reinvested earnings into research and infrastructure. They strengthened oversight bodies rather than weakening them. They prepared successors decades before transition. They did not rely on tradition alone. They institutionalized governance and educated heirs in philosophy and mechanics alike. They went beyond aristocratic complacency into architectural discipline.

To move beyond the aristocrat is to accept that nobility today is engineered stability. It is disciplined multiplication. It is structured leadership that survives volatility. It is the ability to expand influence without surrendering consolidation. It is the ability to transition leadership without fracturing ownership. It is the ability to innovate without dissolving governance.

The Old Aristocrat inherited land. The New Aristocrat inherits architecture. The Old Aristocrat guarded titles. The New Aristocrat guard's structure. The Old Aristocrat relied on tradition. The New Aristocrat relies on doctrine. The Old Aristocrat assumed permanence. The New Aristocrat designs it.

The Rise of the Aristologist built the blueprint. Beyond the aristocrat is about becoming worthy of sustaining it. It is about evolving from inherited status into engineered stewardship. It is about understanding that the crown is not ornamental decoration but structural responsibility.

Beyond inherited privilege lies engineered power. Beyond symbolic authority lies codified permanence. Beyond aristocracy lies architecture.

And architecture is what outlives you.

Chapter Reflection & Strategic Notes
The Rise of the Aristologist

CHAPTER TWENTY-THREE

RAISING ARCHITECTS INSTEAD OF CONSUMERS

Civilizations are not weakened first by invasion. They are weakened by consumption without construction. Families do not collapse first because of external opposition. They collapse because internal discipline erodes. Institutions do not dissolve because markets fluctuate. They dissolve because the next generation was trained to enjoy what was built rather than understand how it was engineered. The Doctrine of Permanent Power cannot survive if those who inherit structure were conditioned only to spend rather than build. The Rise of the Aristologist demands a new educational philosophy inside the household, one that replaces passive consumption with active architecture.

The difference between a consumer and an architect is not income level. It is orientation toward value. A consumer interacts with finished products. An architect studies systems behind them. A consumer evaluates based on comfort and preference. An architect evaluates based on durability and function. A consumer sees opportunity as access to enjoy. An architect sees opportunity as responsibility to design. When generations are raised primarily within consumer culture, permanence becomes unlikely because systems are not respected deeply enough to preserve them.

Modern society encourages consumption aggressively. Advertising reinforces immediate gratification. Social media amplifies lifestyle display. Financial systems normalize debt driven comfort. In such an environment, even heirs to structured institutions can unconsciously adopt consumer thinking. They may inherit consolidated ownership yet lack structural understanding. They may enjoy ecosystem benefits yet fail to grasp the governance beneath them. This is where decline begins quietly.

Raising architects instead of consumers requires intentional conditioning. It requires exposing children early to how systems operate. It requires involving them in discussions about governance, capital allocation, ownership structure, and risk management. It requires teaching them not only what the family owns but why it was structured in that way. It requires demonstrating that distribution channels, intellectual property consolidation, and holding frameworks are not abstract legal decisions but strategic shields protecting permanence.

An architect mindset is cultivated through participation rather than lecture. When children observe negotiations, they learn leverage. When they review financial reports, they learn discipline. When they attend governance meetings, they learn accountability. When they witness strategic decision making across multiple entities, they begin to understand ecosystem thinking. Exposure builds structural intuition.

The New Aristocrat must understand that infrastructure does not appear by accident. Direct to consumer channels require strategy. Brand equity requires disciplined consistency. Intellectual property requires protection. Consolidated ownership requires foresight. Without this understanding, inheritance becomes fragile.

There is also the matter of emotional training. Consumers react emotionally to fluctuation. Architects respond structurally. When markets decline, the consumer fears loss. The architect evaluates adjustment. When public opinion shifts, the consumer seeks validation. The architect reinforces the foundation. Raising architects requires teaching emotional steadiness during volatility. It requires modeling discipline under pressure.

History demonstrates clearly that generational erosion often begins when heirs disconnect from the operational realities of the enterprises they inherit. Distance breeds abstraction. Abstraction breeds carelessness. Carelessness breeds fragmentation. Families that preserved authority across generations embedded heirs within the system early. They rotated them through departments. They educated them formally in finance and governance. They instilled humility through responsibility rather than entitlement.

The Doctrine of Permanent Power cannot be sustained by individuals who seek comfort above continuity. It requires successors who see stewardship as identity. It requires individuals who instinctively ask whether a decision strengthens architecture. It requires discipline to reinvest rather than extract excessively.

Raising architects also means redefining success within the household. Success cannot be measured solely by visible wealth. It must be measured by alignment with doctrine, by understanding of structure, and by contribution to ecosystem strength. Recognition should reinforce discipline, not indulgence.

This educational process is not harsh. It is empowering. Architects operate with confidence because they understand the blueprint. Consumers operate with dependence because they rely on systems they do not comprehend. Understanding builds responsibility.

The future will challenge institutions with unprecedented complexity. Artificial intelligence, digital currencies, global supply chain volatility, regulatory shifts, and rapidly evolving consumer behavior will test structural resilience. Heirs raised as consumers will struggle to adapt strategically. Heirs raised as architects will adjust systems while preserving consolidation.

The Rise of the Aristologist created doctrine. Raising architects ensures that doctrine survives.

When children are taught to create rather than consume, to design rather than drift, to steward rather than spend, the cycle of restart is broken. Architecture becomes generational instinct rather than temporary discipline.

The New Aristocrat was not born. He is trained. He is shaped by exposure to governance, disciplined by capital responsibility, anchored in doctrine, and strengthened by structural education.

Raise architects and permanence becoming culture.

Raising consumers and permanence becomes memory.

The Rise of the Aristologist does not end with structure built. It continues with minds formed to protect it.

Chapter Reflection & Strategic Notes
The Rise of the Aristologist

CHAPTER TWENTY-FOUR

THE FAMILY CONSTITUTION AND THE CODE

Every enduring institution in history has one common trait. It writes down what it refuses to lose. Nations draft constitutions to define authority and limit chaos. Corporations codify bylaws to preserve structure beyond personalities. Universities preserve charters that define missions across centuries. Yet many families who control significant assets, brands, intellectual property, and influence operate without written doctrine. They rely on memory, assumption, and goodwill. The Rise of the Aristologist demands more than goodwill. It demands documentation.

A family constitution is not ceremonial language. It is structural protection. It is the translation of philosophy into enforceable architecture. It defines mission, clarifies governance, codifies ownership principles, and establishes succession expectations. Without written structure, generational power becomes vulnerable to reinterpretation. With written structure, direction survives emotion.

The Family Constitution begins with mission. It must articulate clearly why the family exists as an institution beyond bloodline. It is the purpose of preserving generational capital.

Is it expansion of economic ecosystems? Is it community influence? Is it intellectual leadership? The mission becomes the anchor that guides decision making when complexity increases. When future generations debate strategic direction, the constitution becomes a reference point rather than an opinion contest.

The second pillar of the constitution is governance. Who votes? How are major decisions approved? What threshold is required for asset sales? How is leadership selected? How are disputes resolved? These questions cannot be left ambiguous. Ambiguity breeds conflict. Clarity breeds stability. Governance transforms emotional disagreement into a procedural process.

The Code operates alongside the Constitution. The Constitution defines structure. The Code defines behavior. It articulates expectations regarding discipline, stewardship, confidentiality, public representation, and alignment with doctrine. It clarifies that ownership carries responsibility, not entitlement. It reinforces that public conduct reflects institutional identity.

Historically, families that survived centuries operated with implicit codes even when not formally written. Merchant families maintained internal rules regarding marriage alliances, capital reinvestment, and succession training. However, in the modern era of legal complexity and digital exposure, implicit codes are insufficient. Documentation is protection.

The Family Constitution must also address ownership consolidation. Equity must be layered intentionally to prevent fragmentation. Voting rights must be defined clearly. Transfer restrictions must be documented. Without these protections, generational expansion multiplies instability. When ownership is centralized strategically within holding structures, alignment strengthens.

Succession planning is another essential component. Leadership roles must not be assumed by age alone. Competence criteria must be defined. Evaluation mechanisms must exist. Mentorship pathways must be integrated. Transition must be gradual and documented. Sudden transfer without preparation destabilizes confidence.

Capital discipline must be codified as well. Distribution policies must be clear. Reinvestment ratios must be intentional. Debt tolerance must be defined. The Constitution ensures that financial decisions align with long term compounding rather than short term extraction.

The Code reinforces cultural continuity. It clarifies that governance meetings are mandatory, not optional. It establishes confidentiality expectations to protect intellectual property and strategic advantage. It requires educational participation for heirs. It defines public representation standards to preserve brand credibility.

The New Aristocrat does not resist documentation. He demands it. He understands that what is not written is eventually rewritten by circumstance. He recognizes that clarity today prevents fracture tomorrow.

The Family Constitution also creates emotional stability. When disputes arise, individuals can refer to agreed principles rather than argue from memory. It reduces personalization of disagreement. It strengthens unity by anchoring discussion in doctrine.

Looking toward the future, generational complexity will increase. Families may operate across industries, jurisdictions, and continents. Regulatory environments will evolve. Digital assets will require specialized oversight. Without written governance, confusion will escalate rapidly. The Constitution becomes a navigational map in uncertain terrain.

The Rise of the Aristologist emphasized designing what cannot be erased. The Family Constitution is one of the most powerful tools to achieve that permanence. It transforms philosophy into framework. It turns alignment into architecture. It converts aspiration into documented authority.

The constitution is not rigid. It is reinforcement. It can be reviewed periodically. It can evolve responsibly. But its core principles remain anchored in doctrine.

Write what you refuse to lose. Codify what you intend to preserve. Document what you expect to endure.

The family that writes its constitution secures its direction.

The family that neglects it risks starting over.

The Rise of the Aristologist becomes generational when the Constitution is written, practiced, and honored.

Chapter Reflection & Strategic Notes
The Rise of the Aristologist

CHAPTER TWENTY-FIVE

AUTHORITY WITHOUT CHAOS

Authority is indispensable to leadership, yet history has shown repeatedly that authority alone does not guarantee stability. It can guide, enforce, and protect, but when it is not anchored to structure it becomes volatile. The Rise of the Aristologist does not reject authority. It refines and disciplines it. Authority must operate within governance, not above it. It must be shaped by doctrine rather than personality. When authority exceeds documented boundaries, instability begins quietly. When authority is embedded within architecture, permanence strengthens across generations.

Throughout history, institutions have collapsed not because they lacked strong leaders, but because leadership operated without constraint. Political regimes built around dominant figures fractured when succession arrived because no structural mechanisms existed to transfer power peacefully. Corporations driven by charismatic founders without independent oversight faltered when crisis revealed unbalanced decision making. Family enterprises governed by one central personality often faced fragmentation the moment that personality was removed. Chaos rarely erupts overnight. It accumulates slowly when authority functions without accountability, when decisions bypass process, and when governance becomes optional rather than foundational.

Authority without chaos requires leadership to be institutional rather than personal. It must be clearly defined, documented, and bound by agreed frameworks. Operational leadership must be distinguished from ownership rights so that daily execution does not override strategic stewardship. Strategic authority must be separated from emotional impulse so that governance remains intact during moments of pressure. When these distinctions are blurred, confusion follows. Confusion invites conflict. Conflict, when unmanaged, invites erosion.

The Aristologist understands that structure protects authority as much as it protects the institution. Governance bodies, councils, and boards are not obstacles to power. They are stabilizers. Defined voting thresholds prevent impulsive decisions from destabilizing long-term direction. Recorded minutes preserve institutional memory. Financial oversight reinforces transparency. Conflict resolution mechanisms transform disagreement into process rather than fracture. Authority becomes predictable rather than arbitrary, and predictability becomes the foundation of trust.

Trust is the invisible currency of permanence. Employees remain confident when leadership decisions follow documented procedure. Partners remain loyal when contracts and governance frameworks are respected. Family members remain aligned when roles and expectations are clear. Authority without structure weakens trust because it introduces uncertainty. Authority within structure strengthens trust because it reinforces reliability.

There is also a psychological dimension to authority that cannot be ignored. Power can inflate ego when not tempered by accountability. Leaders who equate authority with personal superiority often begin to override governance mechanisms in the belief that instinct alone is sufficient. This belief is dangerous. The New Aristocrat recognizes that authority is functional, not ornamental. It exists to preserve continuity, not to elevate personality. It is exercised with discipline, not display.

Historically, leaders who centralized authority without oversight often enjoyed rapid ascent followed by accelerated decline. Without checks and balances, miscalculations multiplied. Without structured counsel, blind spots expanded. Without documented succession, transition became crisis. The lesson is consistent across eras. Authority must be embedded in systems if it is to endure beyond the moment.

Economic ecosystems further intensify this requirement. As enterprises multiply, complexity increases. Brands expand into new markets. Distribution channels are evolving. Regulatory compliance becomes more intricate. Capital flows across diversified holdings. Without defined oversight at the architectural level, operational silos emerge. Financial visibility decreases. Strategic alignment weakens. Authority must therefore operate not merely at the surface of daily operations but at the structural level of consolidation, ensuring that ecosystem integration remains intact.

The Family Constitution and Code provide the framework, but authorities must embody it consistently. Governance meetings must not become ceremonial. They must remain active forums for oversight and alignment. Succession planning must not remain theoretical. It must be practiced deliberately. Financial reporting must not be optional. It must be systematic. Authority without chaos requires adherence to these rhythms of governance.

In the modern era, public scrutiny magnifies the consequences of undisciplined authority. Social media accelerates perception shifts. Regulatory bodies enforce compliance rigorously. Partners demand transparency and stability. In such an environment, impulsive leadership can destabilize not only internal structure but public credibility. Authority anchored in governance shields institutions from these pressures because decisions are documented, processes are respected, and accountability is embedded.

The ethical dimension of authority is equally significant. Institutions that preserve authority responsibly provide stability for employees, partners, and communities. They create predictable opportunities. They sustain ecosystems of influence. Chaotic authority, by contrast, disrupts livelihoods and fractures confidence. The New Aristocrat recognizes that disciplined authority is not only strategic but moral. It protects more than personal interest. It safeguards collective stability.

Authority without chaos is not passive. It is decisive, but its decisiveness operates within boundaries. It is confident, but its confidence is grounded in doctrine. It is strong, but its strength is disciplined by structure. It does not bypass governance to demonstrate power. It reinforces governance to preserve it.

The Rise of the Aristologist was never about acquiring unchecked control. It was about designing power that survives transition. Authority must therefore function in a way that strengthens architecture rather than undermines it. Leaders must prepare successors while they remain strong. They must delegate strategically. They must mentor intentionally. They must accept that embedding authority into structure is not a reduction of influence but an extension of it.

When authority respect's structure, power stabilizes across generations. When authority overrides structure, erosion begins beneath the surface. The difference is often invisible in the short term but undeniable in the long term.

The New Aristocrat governs intentionally. He understands that structure is not limitation but protection. He recognizes that architecture is not constraint but reinforcement. He exercises authority in alignment with documented governance, consolidated ownership, and ecosystem integration.

Authority is strong when it operates within design.

Authority endures when it serves permanence.

Authority without chaos is the final discipline that transforms power into legacy.

Chapter Reflection & Strategic Notes
The Rise of the Aristologist

CHAPTER TWENTY-SIX

TURNING SUCCESS INTO SYSTEMS

I understand that my responsibility is not simply to achieve success. It is to institutionalize it. I do not measure my strength by what I accomplish in a single season. I measure it by what continues to function when I am no longer in the room. If my success depends entirely on my personal energy, my personal relationships, or my personal intuition, then it is temporary. If it is embedded in structure, it becomes generational.

I inherited architecture. I inherited governance. I inherited consolidated ownership. I inherited doctrine. But inheritance alone does not guarantee endurance. My obligation as the New Aristocrat is to convert every victory into repeatable structure so that what works once again works predictably. I do not allow achievement to remain anecdotal. I study it. I will document it. I systemize it.

When a brand expands successfully into new distribution channels, I do not celebrate growth without analyzing the process that made it possible. What negotiation frameworks worked. What capital allocation strategy was effective? What marketing rhythm generated conversion. Operational oversight protected margins. I document these patterns because they must function beyond instinct. Systems protect insight from being lost when personalities change.

When governance meetings produce clarity, I examine why. Was it the preparation? The documentation. The reporting structure. The voting thresholds. I reinforce those elements so that clarity becomes standard rather than occasional. Structure creates predictability. Predictability creates trust. Trust creates permanence.

I do not allow revenue generation to remain personality driven. Relationships are valuable, but they must be reinforced by documented agreements and diversified pipelines. Direct to consumer systems must be mapped clearly. Customer data must be centralized. Reporting must be consistent. I do not want success dependent on charisma. I want it anchored in architecture.

I understand that my predecessors built the foundation. My task is not to rebuild it. My task is to strengthen it. If a marketing channel performs effectively, I integrate it into documented playbooks. If capital compounding strategies protect growth, I codify them into policy. If ecosystem alignment increases leverage, I formalize coordination processes. I refuse to allow success to remain improvisational.

History has shown what happens when founders fail to systemize brilliance. Enterprises decline during transition because successors inherit inspiration but not instruction. I will not repeat that pattern. I convert inspiration into instruction. I turn strategy into documented procedures. I turn experience into institutional memory.

Systems are not rigid cages. They are stabilizing frameworks. They allow innovation without fragmentation. When operational processes are clear, new initiatives can integrate smoothly. When financial oversight is consistent, expansion can occur without destabilizing consolidation. When reporting structures are disciplined, complexity becomes manageable.

I also understand that success without measurement becomes an illusion. Therefore, metrics must be defined. Review cycles must be regular. Governance oversight must be respected. Capital allocation must follow disciplined thresholds. Systems require accountability. Without it, they degrade quietly.

My responsibility extends beyond maintaining what exists. I must evolve systems to meet future complexity. Technology will reshape markets. Regulatory conditions will shift. Consumer behavior will change. I cannot predict every variable, but I can ensure that architecture is strong enough to absorb adaptation. Systems allow evolution without surrendering consolidation.

I reject the idea that leadership is merely visionary. Leadership is structural. Vision without a system fades. Structure without vision stagnates. I operate at the intersection of both. I innovate within architecture. I scale within governance. I expand within consolidation.

The Rise of the Aristologist built power designed to outlive a lifetime. My role as the New Aristocrat is to ensure that every gain is embedded into the framework, so it does not disappear with circumstance. If we secure new markets, they are integrated formally. If we strengthen brand equity, it is protected legally. If we build community influence, it is reinforced through documented engagement structures.

I do not want success to depend on memory. I want it to depend on the method.

I do not want momentum to depend on personality. I want it to depend on the process.

I do not want to rely on emotion. I want it to rely on engineered rhythm.

Success achieved personally is temporary. Success embedded structurally is permanent.

I inherit architecture. I reinforce architecture. I expand architecture.

Because my responsibility is not to rise again from nothing.

My responsibility is to ensure that we never have to start over.

Chapter Reflection & Strategic Notes
The Rise of the Aristologist

CHAPTER TWENTY-SEVEN

COMPOUNDING INFLUENCE ACROSS BLOODLINES

I do not measure my influence by the applause of the present. I measure it by the alignment of the future. I understand that the true test of architecture is not whether it functions during my lifetime, but whether it strengthens across generations. Wealth can be inherited in a single transaction. Influence must be cultivated and reinforced continuously. If capital compounds through disciplined reinvestment, then influence compounds through disciplined stewardship. As the New Aristocrat, I recognize that my responsibility extends beyond preservation. I am tasked with multiplication across bloodlines.

Financial compounding is often taught in simple formulas. Preserve principal. Reinvest earnings. Allow time to accelerate growth. Influence follows similar laws, though it operates less visibly. Governance discipline compounds when respected repeatedly. Intellectual doctrine compounds when transmitted consistently. Reputation compounds when protected deliberately. Ecosystem alignment compounds when reinforced structurally. The multiplication is not explosive. It is gradual, deliberate, and exponential over time. But like capital, it can reverse quickly when neglected.

I understand that compounding requires continuity. If one generation preserves structure and the next abandons it, growth stalls. If one steward reinforces governance and the next bypasses it, alignment fractures. Compounding is not automatic. It requires intentional discipline across each transition. That is why education within the bloodline is not optional. It is foundational.

I do not assume that inheritance produces understanding. I create exposure. Heirs must sit in governance sessions. They must review consolidated financial reports. They must understand why equity is layered under holding structures rather than dispersed casually. They must see how distribution channels reinforce brand leverage. They must understand how intellectual property consolidation protects long term control. When understanding deepens, stewardship strengthens. When stewardship strengthens, influence multiplies.

History offers clear lessons in both multiplication and erosion. There were merchant families whose influence extended across continents because they embedded discipline into succession. Their heirs were trained in negotiation, capital allocation, and governance long before authority transferred. Each generation reinforced structure. As a result, their influence expanded not merely through wealth but through strategic relationships and institutional credibility.

There were also families whose influence vanished within decades because successors disconnected from doctrine. They inherited assets but not architecture. They inherited privilege but not philosophy. Without understanding consolidation, they fragmented ownership. Without respecting governance, they personalized authority. Without capital discipline, they extracted rather than reinvested. Compounding reversed.

I study these patterns carefully. I refuse to allow repetition of erosion. My stewardship is not passive. It is vigilant.

Compounding influence across bloodlines also requires reputational discipline. Reputation is structural capital. When a family consistently operates within governance, honors commitments, and maintains alignment, trust accumulates. Partners seek stability. Communities recognize reliability. Markets reward consistency. Trust multiplies leverage quietly. However, one generation's recklessness can erode decades of credibility. Therefore, conduct becomes architectural.

I understand that influence extends beyond financial metrics. It extends into narrative. It extends into philosophy. It extends into how the institution is perceived culturally. If doctrine remains clear and aligned, influence strengthens beyond transactions. It becomes identity. Identity multiplies because it shapes behavior consistently.

Ecosystem integration accelerates compounding. When brands reinforce doctrine, doctrine reinforces community, community reinforces distribution, and distribution reinforces capital, each layer amplifies the others. This is not accidentally constructive collaboration. It is designed multiplication. If one layer weakens, the others absorb temporarily, but long-term compounding requires all layers to remain aligned.

I also recognize that complexity will increase with time. Future generations will inherit digital assets, global partnerships, and regulatory landscapes that I cannot fully predict. Technology will reshape industries. Artificial intelligence will transform decision making. Consumer behavior will evolve rapidly. If architecture remains shallow, complexity will destabilize influence. If architecture remains deep and consolidated, adaptation will strengthen it.

Compounding requires humility. I am not the culmination

of this institution. I am a steward within a continuum. My obligation is to leave structure stronger than I received it. The next generation must do the same. That is how compounding operates. Each steward reinforces rather than extracts. Each leader strengthens governance rather than bypasses it. Each heir expands ecosystem integration rather than fragments it.

There is also psychological discipline required. I must resist the temptation to prioritize short term dominance over long term consolidation. Influence that explodes rapidly without structural reinforcement fades just as quickly. Influence that grows steadily within governance frameworks becomes resilient. I choose resilience.

Compounding influence also requires alignment beyond immediate bloodline. It extends to how the family interacts with community, industry, and institutional partners. When relationships are cultivated responsibly and reinforced through consistent conduct, external networks become part of the compounding effect. Influence multiplies outward as stability attracts collaboration.

The Rise of the Aristologist engineered permanence. My role as the New Aristocrat is to ensure that permanence does not remain static. It must expand responsibly. It must deepen structurally. It must adapt intelligently. It must compound deliberately.

I protect consolidation. I reinforce governance. I educate successors. I strengthen ecosystems. I preserve capital. I align the narrative. I discipline authority.

Because influence that compounds across generations becomes culture.

And culture that is architected becomes power that cannot

be erased.

I will not allow the cycle to reset.

I will not allow the foundation to weaken.

I will ensure that what was built does not merely survive.

It multiplies.

Chapter Reflection & Strategic Notes
The Rise of the Aristologist

CHAPTER TWENTY-EIGHT

COMMUNITY AS INFRASTRUCTURE

I no longer see community as something outside of my enterprise. I see it as the soil that determines whether my enterprise survives. I understand now that bloodline architecture, consolidated ownership, disciplined governance, and capital preservation can only endure if the environment surrounding them is stable enough to sustain long-term operation. Permanence is never insulated entirely from its surroundings. If the ecosystem around an institution weakens, instability eventually reaches the core. That is why I have redefined community not as charity, not as philanthropy, not as marketing, but as infrastructure.

Infrastructure allows movement. Roads allow commerce to travel. Ports allow goods to flow. Digital networks allow information to circulate. In the same way, strong communities allow institutions to operate without friction. When communities are economically empowered, educationally disciplined, and culturally aligned with productive values, they reinforce the enterprises embedded within them. When communities are fractured, economically unstable, or disconnected from opportunity, even well-designed institutions must expend energy defending against external volatility. Community strength determines whether architecture can expand or must constantly defend.

History demonstrates that enduring institutions rarely thrive in collapsing environments. Industrial leaders who invested in workforce development, civic institutions, and local economic ecosystems were not merely acting generously. They were reinforcing stability for their enterprises. Merchant families that strengthened guild systems and trade networks were not acting sentimentally. They were reinforcing commercial reliability. Economic power multiplies more effectively when the environment surrounding it is disciplined.

I do not approach community engagement as image management. I approach it as structural reinforcement. When I support entrepreneurial education, I am increasing the number of architects within my ecosystem. When I contribute to disciplined leadership networks, I am strengthening governance culture beyond my bloodline. When I cultivate aligned business owners who understand consolidation and long-term capital discipline, I am stabilizing markets in which I operate.

If I operate within a network dominated by consumption mentality, volatility increases. If I operate within a network shaped by architectural thinking, resilience deepens. Community mindset influences market behavior. Market behavior influences ecosystem durability. Ecosystem durability influences generational stability.

Community is not a crowd. It is a system.

When that system is weak, institutions absorb shock constantly. When that system is strong, institutions expand confidently.

I understand that future economic landscapes will become increasingly complex. Digital decentralization will fragment attention. Economic inequality will generate social tension. Regulatory scrutiny will intensify. Supply chains will shift unpredictably. In such an environment, isolated institutions will struggle. Institutions embedded within disciplined communities will adapt more smoothly.

Community as infrastructure means building economic alignment outward. It means cultivating entrepreneurs who understand capital preservation. It means strengthening local networks that respect governance discipline. It means encouraging ownership rather than dependency. It means reinforcing structural thinking across the environment so that volatility decreases naturally.

When local ecosystems understand consolidation, fragmentation decreases. When communities understand capital discipline, destructive consumption patterns weaken. When leadership culture values governance, instability declines.

Community strength becomes structural leverage.

This also applies culturally. Culture determines behavior on a scale. If culture celebrates consumption without creation, generational decline accelerates. If culture honors discipline, stewardship, and structural thinking, generational continuity strengthens.

I do not want my bloodline to operate in isolation from its surroundings. I want the environment itself to reinforce doctrine. When others understand the value of ownership, governance, and ecosystem integration, alignment expands beyond the family.

There is also reputational capital at stake. Institutions that operate responsibly within community ecosystems build trust that compounds. Trust reduces friction in partnership. Trust strengthens negotiation position. Trust stabilizes influence during controversy. When public perception is anchored in consistent contribution rather than occasional visibility, resilience increases.

However, community as infrastructure does not mean uncontrolled expansion into every social initiative. It requires strategic alignment. I do not invest energy randomly. I reinforce initiatives that strengthen economic discipline, leadership development, and structural education. Infrastructure must align with doctrine.

There is also generational modeling involved. Heirs must witness community engagement not as performative display but as strategic reinforcement. They must understand why alignment beyond bloodline matters. They must see how strengthening local ecosystems protects long-term enterprise stability.

History provides examples of communities that collapsed economically because institutional leadership extracted without reinvesting. The short-term gains were impressive. The long-term erosion was inevitable. When purchasing power declined, markets weakened. When trust eroded, partnerships fractured. Extraction without reinforcement destabilizes ecosystems.

I refuse to extract without reinforcing.

Community as infrastructure is not charity. It is stabilization.

It is the recognition that permanence requires environmental strength.

It is understanding that bloodline architecture cannot flourish in fractured ecosystems.

It is known that influence multiplies faster when

surrounding systems are disciplined.

The Rise of the Aristologist built the architecture of permanence. The New Aristocrat extends that architecture into environment. I reinforce education. I support disciplined leadership. I cultivate aligned entrepreneurs. I protect ecosystem stability.

Because permanence is not secured only by walls.

It is secured by the strength of the ground beneath them.

And when the community itself becomes infrastructure, generational power does not stand alone.

It stands on stable soil.

Chapter Reflection & Strategic Notes
The Rise of the Aristologist

CHAPTER TWENTY-NINE

THE DISCIPLINE OF GENERATIONAL LEADERSHIP

Architecture alone does not guarantee permanence. Governance can be written, ownership can be consolidated, systems can be documented, ecosystems can be aligned, and community can be reinforced, yet all of it remains vulnerable if leadership lacks discipline. Institutions rarely collapse solely because of external opposition. They erode internally when restraint weakens, when vigilance softens, and when authority drifts from doctrine. Generational leadership demands a maturity that exceeds ambition. It requires control of impulse, management of ego, clarity of long term vision, emotional steadiness during volatility, and unwavering alignment with established principles even when convenience tempts deviation. Without discipline at the leadership level, structure becomes ornamental rather than operational.

The discipline of generational leadership begins with a time horizon. Leaders operating at the generational level cannot think in quarters when their responsibility spans decades. Short term acceleration can seduce even the most capable mind. Rapid expansion feels powerful. Immediate gains appear validating. Public visibility creates the illusion that momentum equals permanence. Yet permanence is not measured by speed. It is measured by structural durability. Every decision must be evaluated not only by immediate return but by long term architectural impact. Opportunities that promise rapid profit yet weaken consolidation are not opportunities but concealed erosion. Expansion that fragments governance alignment is not progress but destabilization. Generational leadership requires patience that protects continuity over acceleration that invites fracture.

Ego presents one of the most subtle threats to permanence. Authority can create the illusion of infallibility. Success can inflate confidence beyond caution. Visibility can distort perception until personality overshadows principle. When leaders begin to believe that institutions exist to serve their identity rather than the reverse, governance weakens. Governance weakened becomes consolidation fragmented. Consolidation fragmented becomes permanence destabilized. Ego replaces doctrine with impulse. Impulse undermines architecture. Generational leadership demands humility to recognize that authority is functional, not ornamental. Leadership serves structure. Structure does not serve personality.

History offers repeated evidence of this pattern. Empires declined not solely because adversaries attacked, but because internal discipline eroded. Corporations faltered not only because markets shifted, but because executives bypassed governance frameworks during prosperity. Family enterprises fractured not merely from external pressure, but because standards relaxed when success appeared secure. Prosperity often weakens vigilance. Comfort dulls urgency. Discipline must therefore be reinforced precisely when conditions appear favorable. Oversight must deepen during expansion. Consolidation must strengthen during revenue growth. Success is not justification for relaxed structure. It is reason for intensified vigilance.

Emotional steadiness forms another pillar of generational leadership. Markets fluctuate unpredictably. Public perception shifts rapidly. Competitors innovate aggressively. Regulatory landscapes evolve. Economic cycles compress and expand without warning. Leadership that reacts emotionally transmits instability throughout the ecosystem. Panic at the top cascades downward. Impulsive decisions destabilize strategy. Confidence erodes internally and externally. Generational leadership requires the ability to absorb shock without transmitting volatility. Calm under pressure becomes structural reinforcement. Measured response becomes institutional stability. Emotional discipline protects governance from reactionary distortion.

Delegation also requires disciplined understanding. Founders and strong leaders often equate personal involvement with control. Yet permanence cannot depend on constant personal presence. If operational execution remains centralized in one individual, succession becomes fragile. Generational leadership demands distribution of authority within documented governance frameworks. Mentorship must be intentional. Authority must be layered. Successors must operate within established structure before transition occurs. Delegation is not surrender of influence. It is architectural expansion of capacity. Institutions strengthen when responsibility is shared within disciplined boundaries.

Consistence forms the invisible foundation of generational leadership. Governance meetings must occur even during stability. Financial reviews must remain rigorous during prosperity. Succession discussions must continue even when leadership appears secure. Discipline cannot be activated only during crisis. It must operate continuously. Institutional rhythm builds predictability. Predictability builds trust. Trust builds permanence. When leadership respects rhythm, structure strengthens naturally.

Behavior transmits culture more effectively than instruction. If governance procedures are bypassed for convenience, successors interpret that action as precedent. If standards are diluted for short term gain, future leaders normalize compromise. If consolidation is weakened for expediency, fragmentation becomes habitual. Discipline must therefore be visible. It must be modeled consistently. The tone set by leadership becomes the template embedded into institutional behavior.

Moral clarity constitutes the final layer of generational discipline. Doctrine is not decorative language but an ethical compass. Decisions must align with principle even when compromise appears profitable. Reputation once weakened fractures ecosystems. Trust once broken destabilizes partnerships. Influence once compromised erodes gradually but persistently. Generational leadership requires refusal to trade long term integrity for short term advantage. It requires strength to uphold consolidation, governance, and doctrine even when pressure mounts.

The Rise of the Aristologist established architecture designed to outlive a lifetime. The New Aristocrat protects that architecture through disciplined restraint. Leadership is not measured by visibility but by durability. It is not defined by dominance but by continuity. It is not proven by speed but by stability across transition. When structure strengthens through succession, discipline has prevailed. When governance remains intact beyond personality, restraint has succeeded. When influencing compounds without fragmentation, maturity has been sustained.

Architecture rarely collapses from pressure alone. It collapses when discipline erodes internally. Generational leadership ensures that restraint remains stronger than ambition, that doctrine remains stronger than ego, and that continuity remains stronger than impulse.

Because permanence is not secured by louder leadership.

It is secured by steadier leadership.

Chapter Reflection & Strategic Notes
The Rise of the Aristologist

CHAPTER THIRTY

LEGACY WITHOUT EGO

Legacy has long been misunderstood because it is too often confusing with recognition. Many leaders believe legacy is secured when their names are engraved on buildings, attached to institutions, or repeated in public memory, yet history reveals that memory fades while structure either survives or collapses. True generational permanence is not determined by how loudly a name echoes through time but by how securely architecture functions beyond the presence of the one who built it. The New Aristocrat understands that ego is the final and most subtle threat to permanence because institutions constructed for admiration eventually weaken under the weight of self-importance, while institutions constructed for continuity strengthen across transition precisely because their foundation was never dependent upon applause. Throughout history, leaders who pursued legacy through dominance and spectacle often centralized authority and fused identity tightly to their institutions, equating visibility with durability. Their influence frequently appeared formidable during their lifetime, yet succession exposed structural weakness because systems built around personality struggle once personality is removed. Governance that operates only in the shadow of a dominant figure falters when that figure is gone, and when identity becomes the pillar, architecture becomes secondary. When architecture is secondary, fragility increases. Ego distorts priorities subtly, encouraging decisions that elevate personal prominence rather than reinforce structural durability, and over time that distortion compounds until the institution no longer serves continuity but image.

Legacy without ego requires fundamental reorientation in leadership posture. The institution must exist to preserve doctrine, reinforce governance, consolidate ownership, and multiply stability across generations rather than to immortalize the individual who initiated it. When focus shifts from personal remembrance to structural endurance, decision making transforms. Expansion becomes strategic rather than theatrical, authority becomes disciplined rather than performative, and recognition becomes incidental rather than pursued. The true measure of success becomes whether systems operate seamlessly beyond the founder's voice, whether governance remains intact during transition, and whether successors inherit clarity instead of confusion. Such orientation demands humility of the highest order because it requires acceptance that influence must outgrow identity. It demands willingness to mentor successors who may innovate differently and perhaps even surpass visibility, and it requires comfort with invisibility so long as architecture remains strong. A bridge does not require its architect to stand upon it forever to validate its strength. Its strength is proven when it continues to carry weight long after construction. In the same manner, institutions built without ego demonstrate their power when they endure without constant reinforcement from personality.

Ego seeks validation through speed, scale, and spectacle, yet permanence is reinforced through discipline, governance, and consolidation. Ego centralizes authority because control feels synonymous with security, whereas permanence distributes authority within documented frameworks because structure ensures continuity. Ego reacts emotionally to criticism and pursues affirmation, while permanence remains steady because it is anchored in doctrine rather than perception. When leadership becomes self-centered, instability enters quietly through small compromises justified as necessary for growth, and over time these compromises weaken consolidation, soften governance, and distort culture. Legacy without ego therefore protects institutions from internal rivalry as well, because when leadership is defined by status and prestige succession becomes contested, ambition becomes destabilizing, and governance becomes a battlefield rather than a framework. Conversely, when leadership is defined by stewardship and responsibility, transition becomes procedural rather than personal, authority transfers through structure, and alignment is preserved because doctrine remains central rather than personality.

This principle extends beyond internal governance into public conduct and institutional presence. Organizations grounded in permanence do not obsess over recognition but prioritize substance over spectacle and reinforcement over amplification. They invest in strengthening systems rather than amplifying narrative, and as a result reputation grows naturally through consistency. Trust accumulates not through dramatic visibility but through reliable stability, and influence deepens quietly through disciplined action rather than theatrical announcement. The Rise of the Aristologist introduced a doctrine designed to outlive a single lifetime, and that doctrine cannot remain attached to one personality if it is to endure. It must be teachable, transferable, repeatable, and understood as principle rather than idolized as origin. When successors internalize doctrine rather than revere individuals, permanence compounds because culture shifts from admiration to application. Structural anonymity becomes strategic strength, for systems that function without constant personal reinforcement adapt more easily to change, transition without identity crisis, and remain resilient because they were designed to operate independently of any single voice.

Legacy without ego demands restraint during success and composure during adversity. It requires refusal to dilute consolidation for visibility, fidelity to governance even when unilateral action appears expedient, and alignment with doctrine even when deviation seems profitable. It requires leaders to subordinate personal desire to institutional durability and to accept that the highest form of recognition is structural survival. Legacy is not memory preserved in stone, but continuity preserved in governance. It is not repetition of a name but repetition of disciplined stewardship across generations. When governance survives transition, legacy is secured. When consolidation strengthens across succession, legacy is validated. When doctrine remains clear beyond personality, legacy is fulfilled. The New Aristocrat therefore builds not to be celebrated but to ensure that what was constructed does not collapse when leadership changes. Influence is measured not by prominence but by durability, because permanence is the highest form of recognition and what endures does not require advertisement. It proves itself through survival, through stability, and through silent strength across time.

The final discipline of leadership is surrendering the need to be seen in order to ensure that what is built remains. When ego is restrained, architecture stabilizes. When architecture stabilizes, generations strengthen. When generations strengthen, permanence becomes culture rather than aspiration. The highest form of legacy is not admiration. It is endurance. The greatest monument is not stone. It is a structure that continues functioning long after the architect has stepped away.

Build it strong enough to outlive you.

Lead it steady enough to survive you.

Leave it disciplined enough to never need you.

Chapter Reflection & Strategic Notes
The Rise of the Aristologist

A NEW DAY THAT FULFILLED THE PROMISE

There comes a decisive moment in the life of every generation when intention either dissolves into memory or matures into fulfillment. Throughout history, countless leaders have spoken boldly of change, declared sweeping visions, and announced ambitions that stirred emotion in their time, yet few have architected permanence strong enough to withstand transition. Words can ignite momentum, but they cannot preserve structure. Inspiration can awaken action, but it cannot guarantee continuity. Only disciplined design, sustained stewardship, consolidated ownership, and unwavering alignment with doctrine can carry a promise beyond the lifetime of the one who first declared it. The Rise of the Aristologist was never about personal ascent or momentary recognition. It was about engineering a doctrine powerful enough to interrupt the silent generational collapse that has weakened families, institutions, and enterprises across centuries. It was about identifying the invisible fault lines that cause power to fragment, wealth to dissipate, governance to soften, and ambition to reset with every new generation. It was about replacing assumption with architecture and replacing temporary triumph with durable structure.

For generations, the pattern repeated with relentless consistency. One individual would rise through sacrifice and discipline, build influence through relentless labor, accumulate capital through risk and resilience, and establish authority through vision. The second generation, inheriting both the fruits and the expectations of that labor, would attempt preservation, yet often without full understanding of the architecture that produced the initial ascent. Governance would remain informal. Ownership would remain insufficiently consolidated. Doctrine would remain implied rather than codified. By the third generation, fragmentation would begin quietly. Discipline would weaken subtly. Decision making would become emotional rather than structural. Assets would disperse through unguarded dilution. Momentum would erode. The structure would no longer stand on reinforced ground, and the climb would begin again from lower elevation. This cycle was never destiny. It was the consequence of insufficient design. It was the outcome of ambition without architecture, success without systems, and authority without disciplined governance.

A New Day emerged not through proclamation but through structural correction. It began when governance was documented rather than assumed, when ownership was consolidated rather than scattered, when doctrine was codified rather than remembered loosely, and when leadership was disciplined rather than reactive. The promise was never merely that wealth could be created, for wealth has always been created in cycles. The promise was that wealth could be preserved and compounded without collapse. The promise was not merely that influence could be attained, but that influence could be structured to endure across bloodlines. The promise was not simply that authority could be exercised, but that authority could be embedded within governance so thoroughly that it would not fracture when personalities changed.

The Aristologist defined the blueprint with clarity. Aristology established the doctrine with discipline. The New

Aristocrat embodied the restraint and stewardship required to sustain both. What began as language matured into framework. What began as philosophy matured into documented governance. What began as ambition matured into permanence. The fulfillment of the promise did not arrive in spectacle. It arrived in stability. It became visible when systems continued functioning without reliance on personality. It became evident when succession occurred without crisis. It became undeniable when successors inherited clarity instead of confusion, consolidation instead of fragmentation, and doctrine instead of assumption.

This New Day is not announced with fanfare because permanence does not require applause. It reveals itself quietly in aligned structures that continue operating regardless of market cycles. It is visible in consolidated ownership that remains intact across generations. It is visible in governance frameworks that operate consistently whether markets rise or fall. It is visible in successors who understand doctrine deeply enough to innovate without dismantling foundation. It is visible in ecosystems that reinforce one another instead of competing destructively. It is visible in communities strengthened not by charity but by structural alignment. It is visible in leadership that chooses restraint over impulse and continuity over ego.

The fulfillment of the promise does not eliminate adversity. Markets will fluctuate unpredictably. Technology will disrupt established industries. Cultural values will evolve. Economic cycles will compress and expand. Political climates will shift. Yet architecture built with discipline absorbs disruption differently. It bends without breaking. It adapts without dissolving consolidation. It evolves without abandoning doctrine. It strengthens because it was engineered to withstand pressure rather than simply enjoy prosperity. That is the difference between temporary success and generational permanence. Temporary success celebrates visibility. Generational permanence safeguard's structure. Temporary success seeks dominance. Generational permanence seeks durability.

The Rise of the Aristologist was never intended to create a privileged class defined by inherited advantage. It was intended to cultivate a disciplined standard defined by responsibility. The New Aristocrat does not inherit advantage passively. He inherits stewardship actively. He understands that inheritance without discipline invites erosion. He understands that consolidation without governance invites fragmentation. He understands that influence without structure invites volatility. He does not rely on momentum alone. He reinforces systems. He does not celebrate prematurely. He institutionalizes deliberately. He does not pursue admiration. He pursues continuity.

A New Day is fulfilled when children are no longer raised to consume what was built but to protect and expand it. It is fulfilled when bloodlines no longer begin from zero but from reinforced foundation. It is fulfilled when governance meetings are cultural norms rather than emergency responses. It is fulfilled when capital is preserved strategically rather than extracted impulsively. It is fulfilled when authority is exercised within documented boundaries rather than through personal dominance. It is fulfilled when legacy is separated from ego and anchored in structure.

The promise was never about wealth alone. Wealth without permanence is temporary elevation. The promise was about interruption of decline. It was about breaking the silent generational reset that has repeated itself across centuries. It was about replacing fragility with structure, replacing impulse with governance, replacing assumption with doctrine, and replacing restart with continuity. When that shift becomes generational habit rather than exceptional event, the New Day has truly arrived.

The fulfillment of the promise is not dramatic. It is disciplined. It is not loud. It is lasting. It is not built for admiration. It is built for endurance. It is not sustained by applause. It is sustained by alignment. When structure outlives personality, the promise is fulfilled. When consolidation remains intact beyond transition, the promise is fulfilled. When doctrine continues guiding decisions long after its originator is gone, the promise is fulfilled. When architecture stands firm across decades of change, the promise is fulfilled.

The Rise of the Aristologist was the beginning of structural awakening. The New Aristocrat was the embodiment of disciplined stewardship. A New Day is the condition in which permanence is no longer theoretical but operational. It is the moment when generational collapse is no longer assumed but interrupted. It is the era in which architecture becomes culture and governance becomes inheritance. It is the quiet confidence that what was built does not collapse, what was structured does not scatter, and what was disciplined does not decay.

The future does not begin at ground level. It begins at reinforced elevation. The next generation does not rebuild from rubble. It extends from foundation. The cycle does not reset. It compounds.

The Rise was the vision.

The Doctrine was the framework.

The Discipline was the bridge.

The New Day is the proof.

Build what remains.

Govern what you build.

Leave what cannot be erased.

THE CONVERGENCE

WHY I CREATED ARISTOLOGIST, ARISTOLOGY, AND THE NEW ARISTOCRAT

I did not create these words for attention, recognition, or novelty. I created them out of observation, frustration, and responsibility. Over the years I watched the same pattern repeat itself with painful consistency across families, businesses, and communities. I saw individuals rise through extraordinary sacrifice, relentless discipline, creativity, risk, and vision. I saw them build brands from nothing, accumulate capital against difficult odds, command influence in rooms that once excluded them, and create opportunities where none previously existed. Yet I also saw what followed too often. I saw what happened when that same power was not structured deeply enough to survive beyond the person who built it. I witnessed fragmentation during succession, confusion around ownership, emotional decision making where governance should have existed, dilution of equity that should have been consolidated, and families forced to restart from diminished ground because the architecture had never been formalized. That cycle disturbed me not because it was rare, but because it was predictable. It was not failure of talent. It was failure of structure. It was not lack of ambition. It was absence of doctrine.

I began asking deeper questions that would not leave me alone. Why are we taught to rise but not taught to remain? Why are we trained to hustle but not trained to consolidate? Why do we celebrate scale without first securing governance? Why do we equate income with infrastructure and visibility with permanence? I realized that the issue was not motivation. It was language. We did not possess words that elevated permanence with the same intensity that we elevated growth. We had vocabulary for ambition but not for architecture. We had slogans for expansion but not frameworks for consolidation. If something was missing, it needed to be named. That is where the Aristologist was born.

The Aristologist became my answer to the absence of structural consciousness. It describes not simply a successful person, but a builder of permanence. It defines the individual who refuses to celebrate power until it is engineered, who refuses to accumulate wealth until it is consolidated, who refuses to lead without governance. The Aristologist asks different questions. Is ownership protected? Is succession documented. Is authority embedded within structure rather than personality? Is growth reinforced by infrastructure? It shifts the conversation from visibility to viability and from applause to architecture. It awakened a way of thinking that I knew had to become cultural rather than occasional.

But awareness alone is insufficient. Insight without framework fades. So Aristology followed. Aristology is the doctrine that anchors the mindset. It codifies the architecture of permanence. It formalizes governance before growth, consolidation before celebration, structure before scale, discipline before dominance. Aristology transforms instinct into system and converts wisdom into repeatable instruction. It provides language for generational authority and defines how power can be designed to outlive the one who built it. Without

Aristology, the Aristologist would remain an idea held privately. With Aristology, the idea becomes blueprint capable of being taught, replicated, and institutionalized.

Then the New Aristocrat emerged. This was never about inherited privilege. It was about inherited responsibility. The New Aristocrat represents the generation raised within structure rather than reacting to instability. It describes the leader who understands that inheritance without wisdom leads to erosion and that authority without governance leads to chaos. The New Aristocrat is disciplined rather than entitled. He consolidates rather than fragments. He compounds rather than consumes. He separates ego from legacy and sees community as infrastructure rather than audience. He embodies the doctrine that was architected before him.

These three are not separate creations. They are phases of one movement. The Aristologist awakens the mind to structure. Aristology anchors that awakening into doctrine. The New Aristocrat sustains the architecture across generations. Awareness becomes framework. Framework becomes culture. Culture becomes permanent. Each flow into the next naturally, forming a complete cycle of transformation. When the cycle is intact, the generational reset weakens. When the cycle is adopted widely, collapse becomes interruption rather than inevitability.

I created this doctrine because our community deserves more than momentary elevation. We deserve continuity. We deserve systems that protect what we build and governance that prevent fragmentation. We deserve language that values wisdom above ego and consolidation above applause. Too often success has been measured by how high we rise rather than how long we remain. Too often celebration has preceded structure. Too often power has been used before it was engineered. Aristology corrects that imbalance. It insists that wisdom precedes expansion and that discipline outlasts emotion.

This doctrine is rooted in wisdom, not pride. Wisdom understands that power is fragile without structure and that influence evaporates without governance. Wisdom recognizes that visibility is temporary but consolidation compounds. Wisdom sees leadership as stewardship and that permanence requires restraint. I did not create these words to elevate myself. I created them because the absence of language was producing unnecessary collapse. I created them because permanence demanded vocabulary. I created them because our future demanded architecture.

I believe this will become the doctrine of choice because it answers a question that many have felt but struggled to articulate. How do we stop rebuilding from lower ground? How do we ensure our children begin from reinforced foundation? How do we convert hustle into heritage and revenue into infrastructure? Aristology provides not merely inspiration but instruction. It shifts culture from reaction to design and from consumption to consolidation. In a world defined by volatility, a doctrine built on permanence becomes attractive. In markets shaped by instability, governance becomes essential. In cultures driven by impulse, discipline becomes revolutionary.

This is not a movement of noise. It is a movement of structure. It is not about dominance. It is about durability. It is not about being seen. It is about remaining. When the Aristologist awakens structural consciousness, when Aristology anchors wisdom into doctrine, and when the New Aristocrat embodies discipline across generations, permanence becomes not aspiration but expectation.

I created these words because wisdom required language. I created this doctrine because structure required definition. I created this movement because the future required continuity.

The convergence is complete when awareness becomes architecture, architecture becomes culture, and culture becomes permanence.

Awaken the architect. Become an Aristologist

Made in the USA
Monee, IL
04 November 2026

67378299R00115